Positivities Within the Possibilities

By K Gadi-Carreon

Dedication

To all the people who have helped me become who I am:
dad (Rod), mom (Amelia), my two sisters (Malou and
Imelda) and my only niece (Maika).
My circle of strong women who always lift me up, and my
loyal and dedicated friends who continue to make me proud.
To the loves of my life:
Raymund my supportive and loving husband, my two most
precious peas - Karyn Marie (KC) and Kamryn (Kam), who
are my reasons for living and living in purpose.
To my Faith:
God, who always promised me an interesting journey.
Grateful for all the blessings and allowing me for being me
as you're my way, truth, and my life!
"Hope, Faith, Courage and Tolerance"
"Grateful, Power and Strength"

-K Gadi Carreon

A few words about Kay Carreon:

Shakespeare once wrote to his beloved, "How do I love thee? Let me count the ways!" My adaptation with Kay in mind would be, "How do I admire you, Kay? Let me mention a few of many ways!" The world is overflowing with possibles and probables, but lacking in actuals. People dream a lot, but don't take action. Not so with Kay who epitomizes "the little engine that could." She gets things done, and done well, but never with just herself in mind. Noted for her obvious passion for and commitment to helping others achieve their goals, Kay has parlayed that mindset into achieving her own. That win-win attitude has won her respect from all she engages as her success in business, and in life, is built upon a foundation of the success of others. Unusual? Counter-intuitive? Rare? Perhaps, but it works, and this author, great communicator, teacher, and friend to many is proof positive that the road to self-actualization is paved with sacrifice, giving, selflessness, and intrinsic motivation. Kay's road wasn't always easy or straight, but has been filled with unexpected challenges and countless obstacles. Not a problem! Her optimism is front and center. Her ability to reinvent herself makes Madonna look like the change-resistant cartoon character Hem from "Who Moved My Cheese?" In short, Kay is a role model not only for women, but for all who aspire to maximize their potential.

Ed Iannarella, CHO, President
Stonehenge Consulting Group
Ft. Myers, Florida
(o) 239.481.5586
(m) 717.475.4255
linkedin.com/in/ediannarella ed_i @comcast.net

More about the author

Thank you mom for everything that you do and for all the sacrifices you've made for us. I'm beyond proud of you and all of your achievements thus far. You are the strongest woman I'll ever get to know and your perseverance through your hard work is empowering. You are a force to be reckoned with and I'm thankful to have you as my mom and as someone I look up to and hope become. Love you always.

KC

***

Thank you, mom, for making me food and giving life and a shelter. Congratulations on your book.

Love,
Kam

***

There are few who can do what she has done. From running more than one successful business, traveling the world, competing in California's Olympic culinary team, working with renowned chefs all around the world, teaching financial literacy, and sponsoring and hosting fundraisers in our community. Kay is more than a role model but a true philanthropist at heart.

She is the source of inspiration and has such an empowering way of motivating others. Kay has a go-getter attitude and undeniable enthusiasm for life. She turns her setbacks into comebacks and embraces the challenges she is faced. Her passion to make a difference in the world is admirable and she strives to exemplify that every day with her family. Her resilience and dedication to her work coupled with her dynamic disposition is what sets Kay apart from the rest. She is surely a force to be reckoned with and a jack of all trades!

Love you Tita Kay. Thanks for being my aunt, my friend, my role model!

Love,
Maika

***

Kay is the most positive person I have ever met. She is my positive coach and she always brings out the best in me.

Maria Palmore

***

My loving sister with a heart of gold. Nothing can get in their way of her ambition. This book is a memoir of her positive mind and her ability to overcome adversity every step of the way.

Love, Imelda Ball

***

Kay is a loyal friend. She has a cup full of surprises, talented and inspirational. She is all about positivity and growth to cultivate a healthy lifestyle!

Love, Joy Cole

***

Positivity is a choice. It's a mindset that reaps reward when applied to daily life. Positive people choose to focus on the good amidst the bad, and Kay Carreon is one of those people who excel at this. She has always impressed me with her positive outlook on life, seeing the beauty in all things and all circumstances. We need more people like her in today's world!

Cheers, April Locy

***

If there's anyone whom I admire for a person's happy outlook in life, it is Kay. Ever since we were classmates in our primary years through high school in the Philippines, she was already a ball of happiness. In class and outside, you would know when Kay is present because you can hear her distinctive laughter and animated story telling. Looking back, her happiness is anything but shallow – it was coming from an innate positivity. Even at young age, she was already finding the good in every person, in every situation, in every possibility.

We lost touch for close to two decades after high school – we went to different colleges and she pursued a career in hotel and restaurant management and moved to California, while I became a full-time broadcast journalist and part time college professor in the Philippines. When we reconnected in the mid 2000's, she was the same Kay I knew, but even happier, more successful and deeply authentic.

I moved and settled down with my family in California in late 2011. By 2014, I was in rut as a migrant, things were not as I wanted them to be, life was slow for me who was used to the fast-paced days in the newsroom, the excitement of field reporting and just, achieving. Unsure where I was personally headed at that time, I knew I needed changing but one thing I was sure of was that I was bent on staying in the US, for my family.

An excerpt from the book I read 'Eat, Pray Love' by Elizabeth Gilbert, resonated to me at that time: 'When you sense a faint potentiality for happiness after such dark times, you must grab on to the ankles of that happiness and not let go until it drags you face-first out of the dirt – this is not selfishness, but obligation'. And I thought about Kay's positive outlook in life too. Awe inspiring and contagious. I wanted that for me, and told myself it wouldn't hurt to try something, no matter how miniscule of a step it might be. So for every day, for 100 days in the last quarter of 2014, I listed one positive thought or anything I was grateful for in my life. I didn't only write them down; I manifested them and socially blasted each one by posting anything that made me happy, big or small, every day for 100 days, #msgoldjoys, #100happydays.

Turns out, that little thing, was life changing for me. Heck yeah, really good things started happening for me and my family. I got promoted, we bought our first home and also among many blessings, I started my new financial planning business too – with Kay whose leadership and guidance to them REACH Insurance team has just been both inspirational and aspirational.

So yes, this book's author, Kay Gadi Carreon is as positive as an influence as she truly is. I'd be one in perhaps hundreds she has met and whose lives she's touched with her authenticity and positivity. If it is something you'd also wish for yourself, this book is for you. Indeed, there is an art in finding positivity in every possibility. And it is that kind of positivity that breeds gratefulness, which in turn channels life-long happiness. Staying positive amid all of life's chaos is a conscious choice and needs constant effort. And there's an art to it, which Kay has truly mastered.

- Marigold Haber-Dunca lives in California with her family. She is a commercial property manager, licensed in real estate and financial planning, former broadcast journalist and college professor in the Philippines

Table of Contents

Foreword

I believe when Kay Gadi was born, she came out of this world with all the positive elements in her whole body. I've known Kay from the time she graduated from college with a degree in Hotel and Restaurant Management. She had her practicum with us and from being a practicumer, she became a significant member of our Le Souffle Restaurant, then the most sought after fine dining restaurant at the heart of Makati's business district. She was my most favorite assistant. Her superb positive outlook in life, her excellent attitude towards work and most especially her extremely contagious crisp laughter made her adored by everybody so that when she bade us goodbye to migrate to the USA, we felt like the world crumbled on us. But look at her now! With all the titles and acronyms attached to her name, I can only conclude that following that direction was really the best for her and her family. She only thinks of greatness, not alone for herself, but especially for everybody she comes across with in life. She only wants the best for people and exhausts all efforts to alleviate their plight, her current profession can testify to this.

I don't see anybody more fit to write a book on positivity than Kay. Her life exudes only positive energies; I think the opposite does not exist in her dictionary! When a person is endowed with so much talent and utilizes those talents to the max, there is no way but up! Kay is an ardent achiever. She knows her role in life and definitely her perfect place in this world. "Life has taught me that possibilities are endless..." as she states in Chapter 1. Learn about the mathematics of relationship in Chapter 2 and come up with an impressive sum! I am glad that she is able to document her desire in inculcating positive mindset as you can find in the succeeding chapters of her book: how to have balance in your life and career, how to know yourself more, how you want people to remember you, the journey to greatness, the right way of loving oneself, etc. If only everybody in this world would find time to read this book, then our world that is full of hopelessness, disgust, corruption, suffering, indifference and hate will definitely be transformed into a world filled with greatness, enthusiasm, honesty, charity, gratitude, and love. And, like Kay, laugh out loud and fill the earth again with everything positive!

I can't help but read and go through each page over and over because each chapter is so essential and valuable to one's positive growth. I like this line from Chapter 12: "Gratitude cleanses your body from all negativity that you garner within yourself and helps unleash the winner's potential!!"

That is Kay for you, she does not just talk! She makes things happen and make sure they happen according to God's plan so she will be able to leave distinctive, unforgettable footprints.

All the best to you Kay Gadi Carreon, the most successful, positive, happy achiever I know!

Jessie C. Sincioco
"The Papal Chef"
President & CEO, Chef Jessie Restaurants

Chapter 1
All About the WHY?

Moving to another country can be quite challenging, especially when adapting to a different lifestyle, the mindset of natives, and culture. Safe to say, there is a lot to be learned when you take that path. It is a slow but vital process - to go through situations, learn, and implement them for better decisions. We can argue that everyone deals with something. Still, as an immigrant, you have to strike a balance between what you know and what you learn in a new environment, which adds to the whole proposition. All sorts of people become part of your life, for better or worse. Many play major roles in shaping who you are now.

The following guidance derives from my learnings and wanting to help others who might be in the same situation as I once was. They have been my core in striving for my goals and maintaining or at least trying to have a meaningful, healthy lifestyle.

Breaking down the W.H.Y

Work through your problems with the W.H.Y.

'W' - depicting the important questions driving every action you take, 'why,' 'what' and 'when.'

'H' - for harmony and the most important one;

'Y' - you.

Even when you are at your lowest and life has pushed you to the edge, keep these factors in mind, and I guarantee that a messy, wound-up string of thoughts in your mind can be untangled.

'W'-Why?

It is about your purpose in life, about all the 'why.' Why do you want to succeed in life and for whom? Personally, for me, 'Why' stands for the people I love and who truly care about me. There have been a few bad eggs in my basket, taking advantage of me not being fully informed and aware thereof there is a purpose behind what I do and the choices I make. I do it for the people who has been my strength throughout. So the question remains, why are you doing what you are doing? For what purpose? It seems like a silly question. Some might say right off the bat, 'Because I do not want to die poor.' or 'I would not have to worry about my bills and mental health only if I have the money.' All these answers are valid and correct, but the truth remains that there is a percentage of people who have it all and are not satisfied with their lives. Because one way or another, they have not accomplished their true purpose. Somewhere along the way, they got off the track.

The focal point here is, strive for whatever you believe in, be it financial stability, balance in life, or a general sense of peace but always question and remind yourself of its importance to achieve it. It's easy to feel lost when you do not have a destination in mind or meaning behind your actions. Remind yourself why you started on your chosen path, your ideas, and where you imagine you will be at the end of the road. Why is achieving a certain position or lifestyle important? Does it give you the purpose and achievement you want in your life? Not fulfilling your

16

core purpose results in the sense of emptiness and loss of fulfilment. Have a dip in your PENSIVE. Dive deep in the ocean of your thoughts and mindset that you started with. It helps in redacting the 'what-ifs' from one's life.

Diverging your mind from all the possible downfalls to keep your mind solely focus on your goal is the healthiest way to opt for. It is not only rewarding for you but the people who rooted for you along the way. Who was there to uplift and help you pull through dark times? The ones who were your mentor or guide when you needed a solid dose of advice and therapy. All of them become a part of your reason. Your purpose in life will be the determining factor of the result. It drives you towards your chosen future. To get most from options available at present and identifying essentialities, making you more resilient despite obstacles.

'W'-What?

The word 'what' is the deciding factor. What should you do to achieve your goal, your 'why,' no matter what? Do whatever you can to get there. As someone who had to adapt to a new place and welcome the ups and downs it brought along, I have learned not to be scared to take up challenges and explore the course of actions. Whatever it is, I know I am stronger than the impediment at hand. Thinking big is scary. Knowing there will be innumerable hurdles while working for those ideas is terrifying. What sets your game plan apart from others is how much you have faith in yourself and planning your ideas accordingly. Having a positive attitude or outlook can work wonders.

Hustling with a healthy mindset will get you there faster and more efficiently. Give yourself the time and space to explore the options. You might not always have favourable conditions. Women usually do not but look how far we have come in that regard as well. Minorities and immigrants most often than not have to comply with policies, whether official or just cultural presets, slowing the pace for them to reach the top. This difference in treatment is usually the cause of the inferiority complex, thinking you might not be as smart or good enough as the others. I can't emphasize this enough. However, even with such conditions, you will still be you. The person who is brave enough to take on the world despite its challenges, not hiding from facing them, not minding what others think of you or your potentialities—not being afraid to put your ideas out there, taking in criticism and guidance from others. Be confident in yourself and what you got for the world. The competition is fierce out there, and the hard reality is that you might not be as skilled as others, but that should not have to be the reason you give up. Seek as much exposure as you can to understand things better. As long as you have the belief and trust in yourself, respect for efforts that you put in, overlooking unnecessary negativity, there is no reason for you to undermine yourself. The journey is as important as the destination, maybe even more.

'W'-When?

Another 'W' is the 'when.' Know that every problem has a solution. Even when at the last resort, understand that you cannot go any lower. The only way is up. Life has taught me that possibilities are endless, even if you have run out of all options. You think you are at the end of the road, and there opens a path you might have overlooked or maybe can create one yourself. Never miss seeing the light at the end of the tunnel. Do not give up on your dreams and aspirations when stuck in an undesirable position. Instead of wasting time and dwelling on how big the obstacles are, direct your energy towards how to solve the problem at hand.

The outcome of being stressed out is ultimately draining yourself for hours and still not coming up with a solution. We have examples of all these amazing people who failed at first, but because they refused to give in, not only did they benefit themselves but the entire world. Thomas Edison had to go through several - reportedly hundred failed attempts before he managed to light up our world with the invention of light bulbs. That does not only apply to entrepreneurial endeavors, of course. Working on and evaluating yourself to grow is an amazing aim. Realizing where we are going wrong and making efforts to improve is the biggest gift we can present ourselves with. Some realize what they want from life early on and work towards it from thereon.

Some do it later, which is fine as well. So do not give up on yourself or your preferred destination. Life is not easy or fair thereof, but you should be aware of your true potential and how you can handle the hard stuff no matter where, what or who throws it at you.

'H '- Harmony

Albert Camus, a French philosopher and recipient of the Nobel Prize in Literature, stated, "But what is happiness except the simple harmony between a man and the life he leads?" emphasizing the connection between oneself and his persuasions. Be in harmony with yourself and your beliefs. Draw a very detailed image of how you want your life to be but make sure to be at peace with it.

'Y'-You

The very foundation, an essential element of the whole process, is, in fact, 'You.' It does start at home. If you do not love yourself, you cannot extrude or share it with anyone else. Be kind to yourself. You are all you have got. Treat your mind and soul with good energy, the way you want others to. Be confident and secure in your skin. When there is no enemy within, the enemies outside cannot hurt you. You will probably be doing others a favor by doing their job of bringing in negativity if you coax yourself in the corner. Do not give way to those ugly thoughts of being useless or unworthy of desired goals. Restraining ourselves from full potential by focusing on wrong variables instead of the 'why' as discussed before. Rather work on your weaknesses and try to overcome them. We cannot turn into a completely different being overnight, but we can try. We can look for solutions to become the person we want to be. All of us are equal.

There is always a choice

Making life-changing decisions is stressful, and rightly so. You can stress all you want if the step you are about to take might seem to be 99 percent a wrong one, but that is the thing about life, for it to continue and to know if it really will be a bad one, you will have to take the step. Holding yourself from potentially making the right decision and turning it into reality might be more of a disaster. To put it simply, if you do not explore an option, you would never be informed about its pros and cons.

What if it does turn out to be a miscalculation? The worst situation would be a failure, but you can only go north to better grasp and understand the circumstances. There will not be any regrets or what could have been, as per your expertise and capabilities. It is wise to embrace what befalls you regardless of the result. There is plenty of trial and error in the process of figuring out 'the right way.'

Human beings would not have developed had we not experimented with ideas in the first place. Thinking of new ways, putting in hard work, if the outcome is not desirable, we can have another go and come up with better ones. Bottom line, the harder you fall, the stronger you will bounce back! It all depends upon your energy, your approach, and your PURPOSE.

Conclusion

Wherever you go, as long as you have that 'why,' you can be successful no matter what aspect of life you are striving for. The basis of your actions influences how well your plan works. Being uncompromising and resolute for your aims helps in proficiency and dexterity, which might not be there in a design with no backbone, to begin with.

Aspiring for the best you can have is a spirited thought. To venture into building space or life for oneself comes with difficult choices and greater challenges. Though the result might not be the one you wanted, the process does offer the gain of knowledge for a better life with hope and harmony with your initial resolution in sight.

Chapter 2
Equation of Life

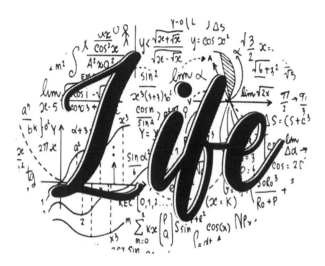

L ife itself, in a way, is a culmination of our relationship with others. We have to calculate carefully the significance and what others offer us for them to be included in our life. Forming one's circle is like formulating an equation of life. Do not worry, for this is not your calculus class, but it is more or less simple math.

Let's discuss this equation of life, shall we? You would want an 'addition' of people who would stick with you through thick and thin. Subtracting the ones who have nothing to offer but negativity, multiplying the numbers of those you could be on the same page, one way or another, and dividing based on your mutual interests. Working around it may take time and courage, but in the end, it will only benefit you.

Addition +

Coming to the US and having lived here, I met many different people from different caste, creed, and color. Anywhere you go, you will add people to your life, be it through your workplace, school, or even your neighborhood. I was quite surprised when I got along with people who seemed strangers at first, and now we are as good as two peas in a pod. You will meet new people and most often than not become acquainted. What's important is that you keep the ones who have a positive approach towards life and the people around them.

People who are a source of inspiration, even on the days when everything seems to be going down, will come up with ideas and move the project onwards. Thinking through loopholes and bringing in optimism can aid in elevating the dark mood, thoughts, and out of tight-knit situations.

Peers who are in the same situation as you can be a great source of motivation. Since you go through the ordeals of every day together, they can understand you better, empathize with your situation and be in sync with your feelings. They might be your competition, so seek out the ones who play it fair and with good spirit.

A friend's eye is a good mirror, so if you have someone who has a habit of agreeing along with whatever you say, chances are he or she is not the best adviser. A 'friend' would make sure to suggest and advise with the best option, no matter how harsh. He/She does not shy away from showing you your true self, and if there is a need for improvement, he/she will tell you so.

People who are always willing to guide you through mentoring, giving alternative ways when stuck in a pickle, uplifting after a bad decision or outcome, and encouraging you to get more out of life because they know your worth. You could confide in them. Take guidance when you do not know where to go. They will direct you in the right direction improving your personal and career life because they have been in the same place before.

Individuals who offer emotional support and are a physical manifestation of 'friend in need is a friend indeed.' That is where authenticity and complete trust lies for you. They might be old friends or new ones who seem to speak the same language as yours. They have mental capability through and through. They do not judge or have a holier than thou attitude. They will listen to all your problems and tantrums, too, just for the sake of you and your mental state.

All relationships work with a 50:50 ratio, give and take, yin and yang. Therefore, if you are lucky to have such individuals' presence, make an effort to add or keep them and offer them the same energy as they do.

Subtraction –

There should absolutely be no space for people who do nothing to nurture you. They are apparently only there to pick up on your weaknesses and spread negativity. There is a clear line between expressing your opinion and right out hurting sentiments. The people who do not respect that line should not be in your circle because their only role is to take you down.

Trying to fit in, especially in a new environment, is already nerve-wracking. Social anxiety takes over and puts the cherry on top by forcing their negativity on everyone else. Filter the bad apples from your basket. It is a hard task that needs to be done for internal peace and mindfulness.

Individuals who walk around with negativity and toxicity - remove them from your life because they do not have anything to offer you except a cold attitude. They can't help it! They end up putting you down and constantly remind you of the failures. Their purpose becomes talking behind your back, making sure everyone hates or does not look at you favorably. Almost bullying you in a depressive state.

A friend or a good-hearted person would never hurt you. Words have the power to make or break us. The psychological effect they have is intense. It does not just change others' perspectives on us, but even we begin to think of ourselves the same way.

The one who claims to be your buddy but never shows up in times of need is NOT your friend. The ones who appear once in a blue moon for their own convenience are NOT your friends. They always seem to be 'busy' when you need them the most. Even if they do bless you with their presence, they usually have something to ask of you. It really makes you question if you are just there for their use and make you feel guilty if you end up judging them wrong. Actual friends or acquaintances would at least try to be there for you and its shows as well.

There are people you trust who have a simple purpose towards you -- demeaning your interests or killing your vibe. Suppose you recommend ideas, concepts or anything. In that case, they will pass it as outdated, not in the trend, or not on par with their intellectual standards. Having a preference is fine but making others feel bad about their choices is not fine at all. If those choices are somehow bad influences, that can be conveyed politely. Again, words matter, and they matter a lot!

Feeling nervous or uncomfortable around someone is a clear sign of why he/she should not be in your circle. You do not look forward to meeting them again because they make you feel unsettled whenever you meet them. It is more of a relief not seeing them than missing them.

People who are uncompromising on accepting others' ideals, those who are not willing to respect or those who are close-minded with regards to ideas shared by others should not be your friend. Their inflexibility makes it hard to work with them. They fail to comprehend that it is a shared experience and all expressions matter. Your circle should consist of people who respect and value your expression and are always willing to uplift and root for those ideas.

There is always a difference in one's intentions. Do they have good or bad intentions towards other's well-being and progress? Suppose they only think about themselves draining the room's positive energy. In that case, honestly, there is no need for such negativity in your life.

Multiplication x

What I have learned from life is that if you do the right thing, think like others or share the same mindset, the tendency of that 'addition' multiplies. You meet a person who has a lot in common with you. Chances are that person will have a whole group of individuals with the same interests, and they might invite you over to their plans or hangouts next time you meet with them. We as human beings have a variety of hobbies that we love to divulge ourselves with, and we all have different ideologies that we live by. What if you can obtain a group for yourself with each hobby, interest, or shared ideology? You simply network with people with commonalities and multiply on good people and invest in strong relationships.

Division ÷

You multiply the same group of people but with different aspects or variables. I have different circles of friends based on my various hobbies and ethics. I have a set I go shopping with, another one I enjoy drooling over delicious meals with, a circle I can confide in, a group I can seek career counseling from, and how to improve it. It is hard or nearly impossible to have all of my circles putting interest in my affairs. Even expecting two of those groups to get together and be able to meet eye-to-eye is unachievable. One cannot associate with different circles at the same time because their thinking will be different. The way I have perceived things, you can and should go for the best, but there will be people who might be happy and envious of you at the same time. It could be over any variable, small or big. That is another reason I believe dividing positively.

Conclusion

How you frame your lifestyle and the people involved in it is up to you. It also serves as a reflection of our relationships which play a major part in establishing where we stand in our lives. Figuring out how we can invest in our time meaningfully while living in this world to the individuals who truly deserve our energy and time.

27

Individuals who are willing to accept us for who we are. It provides a space where you can voice your thoughts without feeling anxious about being judged or put down. Maybe it would take time to come up with the right equation, but it would be worthwhile when you do.

Chapter 3
How Can I Achieve Balance?

The phenomena of 'balance' can be explained as the perfect ratio or percentage of 'give and take.' Whether it is relationships, health, wealth, time management, or just about anything in life. I like to think of it as one should always maintain an equilibrium with how they should give their energy and how much should be received. Thinking and basing your actions on ethical values, not only for others but yourself as well. If one cannot achieve or realize how to balance himself/herself, how can he/she be expected to work around that path for others? Understanding who or what can really make us be optimistic or having a cheerful disposition are ways in keeping our mind neutral.

We usually fail to do so because we give more time to one component and less to others. We exceed one and fall short for the other. While both of them might be beneficial, it can turn into something disputable if sided with one too much. It is hard to treat everything on the same footing, but it can be attained if we try to introduce and implement a few amendments in our daily life.

Important to note: Balance is a constant process - not the final outcome of our lives, but the journey itself.

Self-reflection and call to action

To establish a balanced life and have a strong assessment of your present structure, routine is required. Reflecting on how you handle your personal and work life and seeing what changes are needed is necessary. Feeling like you're not progressing or simply stuck because of mental and physical exhaustion. The results are not as satisfactory as they should be, based on your effort and time spent. This shows there might be factors that are being overlooked and hindered in having a balanced life. This calls for a decision to have things reconsidered and apply them differently.

The theory of 'enough' and putting up boundaries

While it is good to have an achieve-it-all attitude, it is imperative to know when you are pushing yourself, body and soul, to the limits. Accepting when you need to stop, going above what you can give or over doing for others just to please them is not a way of living life for yourself as you don't need to please everyone all the time. You really only got yourself. Do not utilize your resources for other people so much that you run out and have not enough left for yourself. Allow this understanding that you cannot always be there for others and manage every single task for them all the time. Do as much as you can without being excessive. Sometimes, 'enough' is actually enough. I learned this the hard way, of course. Allowing your mind to process the idea that setting boundaries is not wrong, you're doing it in the capacity that you're helping that is within what you can give. We are, after all, just human beings and need to emphasize the matter of 'enough.'

There is a difference between aiding people in time of need or for your own sake and doing a favor for them for the 100th time in a week. What usually happens when someone asks you for something you do not really feel up for? Try to work around, throw in some excuses but eventually give in to the pressure without even being given the time to think about the favor at hand.

You have every right to say 'no' to them without feeling bad when not wanting to go for it. You need to know you cannot be taken advantage of because you are a good person and are willing to help others. Some people tend to ask or rather impose the 'help' without giving a second thought to your situation and your consent. Which makes it all the more of a reason to not give in. Master the art of saying 'no' and equip yourself with a less stressful and more mindful life.

Balance in health

Being negligent with your health is the worst way to push your body off balance. Not being sincere to it would make you unbalanced, quite literally. Unfortunately, health is probably the last thing you think about in today's fast-paced world because there are so many other things that have taken over as priorities. When in truth, it is the foundation of the whole cycle. We cannot grow if our mind and body do not get their due attention or can accomplish anything if we are not strong enough. Being balanced with things that have a direct effect on you is essential. A strict diet or having obesity both have the same bad result. Crazy body workouts or not exercising at all both can cause problems. Keeping on the extreme side will have a bad effect on you one way or the other. We do not consider the effects of such practices, especially at a young age, but as time passes, they catch up in the form of disease or some other ailment. Therefore, adjust to routines that provide both nutrients and strength without bringing harm to yourself. A healthy individual warrants better results and decisions.

Mental health - an essential factor to reaching balance

Mental health is just as important as your physical health. Maintaining your mental health will greatly impact how you function, interact with people, and ensure reaching your balance. There are many factors on which these thoughts are based on - environment, people around you, and how you cope with things. Have these two schools of thought met halfway? You can make healthy combinations - walks in the park while talking to a friend, reading your favorite book or streaming shows while eating healthy snacks, maybe taking a break from work and going on a trip just to have that burden off for some time and vent your problems. Filtering people and deciding who could stay around you is a great way of lessening negativity. People suffering from mental illnesses have a lot on their hands. Not many are brave enough to talk about them because it might mean sharing about their traumas. Seek professional therapy and guidance if you feel like it is hard to keep things together.

If you are on the other extreme and lock up your emotions or are the type to put your load on others, not only will you make others avoid you, but it will also harm your personality. Life is hard, but that does not mean we make it miserable for us to succeed. Maybe you do not have bad intentions or do it unknowingly. You could always learn to be considerate about your words and actions. We all have been through good and bad times. I would know because, like everyone else, I have been there too. Lesson here? Always be kind. Create the perfect harmony between positive thoughts and what your instincts tell you. So you could possess the ideal amount of yin and yang energy to be mentally stronger and more capable of taking on the world.

Balancing the scales of relationships

Our lives revolve around so many relationships, family, friends, colleagues, kids, neighbors, a shopkeeper at the end of the road, and the list goes on. We all play different roles in someone's life. Depending on their relationship with you, maintaining a strong bond with all those people is important. I mean, I would not want to get on the bad side of my grandparents. Try forgetting to call them on festive occasions and birthdays and be nagged for the rest of my life. Even the persons at the grocery store are not the guardian of my food supply. I will not want them shutting the doors at my face if I walk in a minute before the store closes. My point is, the connection between you and your beloved or respected individuals has to have that stable interactive support. We can't disregard that everyone has to carry the weight of the situation. Some can weigh us down but some can bring us up. Our goal is to balance the scale. Of course, the same can be said about the situation where you are the only one carrying it. This transfer of energy and efforts will break through if the quantum is out of proportion. To put it simply, both sides need to give and take equally. From my perspective, humility is the key. No matter where you are in your life, always keep that fine balance.

Conclusion

Balance in all walks of life for me is like inhaling and exhaling - a stable flow that keeps us alive and a vital element of our existence. You have to take the initiative to find the right balance. Whatever you do, be humble about it, somewhere in between being ravenous and ascetic. Always be in sync, in symmetry with the flow of energy. Never too much and never too less. It might feel as hard as trying to keep an eggshell together after it cracks. Still, if you can keep it together, you will be met with loads of appreciation in return, not only for your wonderful act but for having the courage to surpass such a difficult ordeal.

Chapter 4
Having a Wealth Mindset

No one aims for small. Everyone wants to make it big, but what really sets those who do apart from those who cannot do so? The way we think about our goals plays a major factor here. How much you work for it and how much time has been put into planning and execution is vital. Your ethics and mindset are partially responsible for the outcome. It is important to have a strong, clear, and positive mindset towards achieving them while studying ways and critically analyzing them. Setting out with an unclear and negative mind puts you at a disadvantage from the start.

Positive mindset (Focus on what you want and take a step)

Developing a positive attitude toward your efforts, time, aims, and faith in yourself to obtain them is essential. Harboring thoughts of not being good enough for one's goals or being worthy of the good things in life brings discomfort and negativity. All of us deserve prosperity and should have an optimistic outlook of earning sustainability. What life has taught me is to never shy away from the things I want despite continuously being pushed down as if I do not have the right to a better life. Constant failures tend to make one question if they really are worthy or competent enough. To not give in to those thoughts and still have respect for yourself and your dreams is the way to go. If you want something in life, charge ahead with the belief that you can accomplish it, rather than being timid and thinking about it as this big unachievable task. Do not lower yourself.

Working around fears

It is easy to be overwhelmed when setting out or even thinking about achieving your goals. The moment we think about how big or difficult they seem, all insecurities and fears pour in. Anything that could possibly go wrong passes by, just like some sort of film reel in front of your eyes. The thing to point out here is, all those problems that 'you' just made at that moment of overthinking and stress might happen or might not. You are not giving yourself a chance to try or test yourself. Your feeling of fear kicks in and you limit yourself immediately. What if that something can lead to a great success? It is absolutely normal to think and plan ahead, measuring the pros and cons. But to give up entirely just because you could already see some of the obstacles you might face is not the best idea.

Be honest

Be honest with yourself and what you want. Know who you are, where you stand, and where you like to be. You are the only person you can really count on. So be as candid as you can with yourself. It will help you explore yourself and lead you to where you are and actions that will lead you to your destiny.

Assertive approach

Demand that your wants be met, not only from others but yourself. You are not selfish when you bring forth your needs. You balance your assertive attitude when deriving affirmative energy. Be self-assured, all the while being considerate of others.

Become goal-oriented:

Commitment

Commitment is the key to success. Devoting yourself to your goals, whether big or small, will aid in making you more goal-oriented. Sure, you have an idea but are you truly dedicated to it? Are you working night and day to turn your dreams into reality? Unless you are all for it, there is little chance it will manifest. There is no shortcut to success. You have to put in every bit of physical and mental energy for it to materialize. No goals or great businesses have ever been set up by just sitting around and hoping for miracles or things to just fall into place by themselves. As they say, 'A goal with no plan is just a wish.'

Strategic planning

The first step is to plan and be proactive about it. It is of utmost importance to have your tasks planned out. This helps in checking your progress and organizing what needs to be done. There are plenty of distractions throughout your day. Without a firm plan, it is easy to get lost and go off track. There is no saying that you will meet and get everything done as planned. Still, you will have some percentage of work and productivity done, bringing you closer to the desired outcome.

On the other hand, if you have no plans and leave everything to chance, you would end up trying to make up for it and delay the outcome. Therefore, planning is a must.

Be it setting up smaller tasks or bigger ones, be it a day or months. Schedule your time. It helps enormously when you know how to divide your time and work accordingly.

Reviewing

The journey towards one's goal is a constant process. You have to continuously review your progress. Setting up one does not attain any favorable results. You have to understand your position mid-process and remind yourself of your end goal, what you need to work on, and put the variables in place for the process to move smoothly. Track your steps throughout to entertain if you are on the right path. Many people lose hope when they do not see any progress. It is because they do not analyze their tactics or moves. Would they had done so, they would have had a better understanding of what they had done and what could have been done to get on the right course of a track.

Putting sub consciousness into work

Engraving your purpose and goals into your subconscious mind by ceaselessly reminding why you had set on for a specific goal is a great way to keep yourself afresh with passion towards it.

Invest in yourself and your skills (Never stop learning):

Learning

The best thing you could invest in is, in fact, yourself; as Benjamin Franklin had stated, '*An investment in knowledge pays the best interest.*' Whatever you spend on it, you will be paid back exponentially. With the amount of knowledge you take in, you will utilize it and employ what you have learned.

The more you work on yourself and learn new skills, the more opportunities arise career-wise and intellectually -

because there is so much to learn about in this world. It has absolutely no boundaries. From self-reflection to world discovery, the possibilities are endless. There is no time or age limit to it. As long as you live, you will be able to learn something new. It does not stop when you leave the environment of educational institutes. There is no formal route to acquire it. One can only succeed in life when you open yourself to newer knowledge. It helps in deepening our understanding of things that we might not completely understand.

Become a better version of yourself:

Learning helps us in upgrading or becoming a better version of ourselves. Whether it be improving our already acquired skills or introducing new ones to add to our portfolio, there is so much to be learned from others' expertise when we venture on attaining a new skill. Not only does it help us connect but grasp the subject better. Everyone has different opinions, and so it helps to see a point from various angles.

Exposing yourself to new people from various cultures helps in comprehending different schools of thought better. This may come in handy when going for jobs where you have to travel a lot and meet individuals from all over the world.

It helps with critical thinking enhancing our ability to solve problems. The more you can grasp a subject, the easier it is to get to its core and manage by analyzing its advantages and disadvantages.

A reader who takes in information every day has more cerebral development than a normal person. His brains stimulate intellectual gathering where there is plenty of opportunities to gain knowledge.

The world is changing every day. New trends and reports come in every day. To be on par with this constant change, one has to be equipped with its ways. It can only be achieved by having yourself updated with it. Schools have to revise their curriculum every few years to teach children with best and about the newest world. Contents based on older information and therefore no longer useful are taken out. This shows if you remain stuck with knowledge from times gone by, it will make you lag behind. Companies prefer candidates who show skills that can be implemented in today's world. Everyone knows how a simple computer works, but what about the advanced technology that has been introduced? No one would want to take up an individual who is not on the same level as this ever so fast-paced world.

Take any successful individual or organization. They would always state having profound knowledge about their ideas or mastering them after long-term study as one reason behind their success.

Investing your time in perceiving the world and its ways would never go wasted. No matter how small or useless a skill or information may seem to be, it will somehow be of benefit or employed.

Think big!

No one said aiming for the stars is delusional. While I might advise you to start off with small goals, there is nothing wrong with thinking big. It is admirable to go for challenges but nothing that cannot be attained. Go after something measurable. Believe you can achieve a wealthy lifestyle and start working towards it in earnest. If your goal is to create a business, then that is your calling. Make every day count and have as much effort put as possible. Think of the big picture at the end of the road. Take into perspective your present situation, envision what you have to strive towards to bring forth change and have that happy ending crystallized. Think of how you can gain strength and make your goal a reality. What is holding you back from making that one big step, and how can you control those factors?

Thinking about your goal should be exhilarating. If you are not excited about it, then it is less likely you will achieve it. Therefore, set a motivational goal that would get you going.

A clear goal-setting helps in gaining it faster. A vague one would leave you confused and probably lost. Have goals planned out properly, so you know your exact strategy and how it will lead to your goal. It is also vital to know that they are achievable and attainable. That it is within your capability.

Do not spend your money - Invest it

Investing your money is a great way to build wealth if the right decisions are made. If put in the right vehicles, you could potentially have strong rate returns. Accumulating wealth through careful, well-thought-out investments is an amazing way to make money work for you rather you working for it. It is a common perception of millionaires that they are frugal. That might be because they know the value of money and might not put it where there is no saying of getting profitable returns. You can grow money over a longer time by investing in vehicles such as life insurance policies that have cash value, bonds or stocks, etc., building wealth over time. Saving for retirement and living off funds through ventures such as real estate can be really helpful. You might even be able to build a start-up through your investments, helping the young entrepreneurs and benefiting yourself when their business takes off.

Conclusion

Maintaining a wealth mindset is important, especially if you think big and want stability in your life. Having a positive and proactive attitude towards your goals, shaping yourself into a goal-oriented personality is all part of assertiveness for financial stability. Always learn new ways to perfect and mold your strategy and yourself to adapt and think critically in time of need. Work around fears that are holding you back from your potential victory. Put up clear and attainable objectives with instructions and planning to achieve them. Make sure you have investments backing you up. Keep in view all the essential steps to become goal-oriented. Keep all these factors in your mind and work accordingly to create a wealthy mindset. Most of all, never lose hope and think big.

Chapter 5
Mindset for Balance

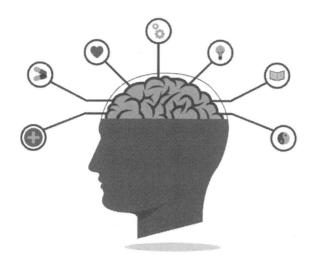

*" *W*e don't need to strive towards balance; we rather need to work on the obstacles that are preventing the natural flow of balance."* —
A.A. Alebraheem

When talking about a 'balanced mindset,' the first thing that comes into a person's mind is finding peace within oneself. It involves being mentally sound and realizing that there is potential for various situations to coexist without overthinking or stressing out. But, before we get into the depths of achieving a balanced mindset, we need to understand what the word 'balance' really means.

According to the **Cambridge Dictionary** definition, "balance is a state of equal weight or force". Looking at this definition more contextually, we can conclude that "balance" is when an individual can have an equilibrium in their life, something that perhaps implies stability and cohesion.

However, when talking about balancing your mindset, one cannot just demand that state of mind to occur. It requires immense patience and acceptance. Recognizing that 'balance' cannot be forced but rather comes naturally might be the first step to achieving it. Although some might dive headfirst into the technicalities – referring to tips and tricks from self-help books to get over their dilemmas.

Often the one thing that pops up in everyone's mind when the topic at hand is mentioned is work and life balance. Most entrepreneurs and employees face a struggle nowadays – trying to allocate strict timings to their respective lives, be it professional or personal.

You cannot avoid unexpected events, no matter how planned you think your life is. Events such as a sudden call from your boss saying you need to work overtime or a date canceling are bound to occur at the very last minute. And no matter how ready you think you are to face them, they do end up messing up your 'perfectly' scheduled timetable.

Work-life balance is a concept where workers must distribute their time equally amongst their leisure activities and work-related activities. It has proven to be a big challenge for the working class to achieve such a balance and remain happy at the same time.

According to Maslow's hierarchy of needs – self-actualization is the greatest form of achievement for a person. To achieve that, they would always want to strive for the best. Forcing the concept of a work-life balance in such a situation will lead to more stressful circumstances than a balanced lifestyle.

A balanced mindset, I believe, is all about creating and getting the most out of your experiences. Being optimistic in situations will lead to having meaningful and memorable encounters.

But how exactly does one achieve this 'balanced mindset'? As claimed by A. A. Alebraheem, an individual needs to recognize the barriers preventing them from accomplishing a certain goal rather than just laying out a very extensive and wishful plan.

Identify your stressors

Acknowledge what it is that is causing hindrance in attaining your goals. One needs to sit down and analyze the things or situations that cause them stress and make a list. Making a hierarchy of the stress-inducing situations would be advised. This way, you would know what needs your utmost attention.

Once the stressors have been figured out and ranked, you can now brainstorm how to go about and resolve them.

Realize that your concepts might differ from others

People often go after the textbook concepts, wanting to have the same ideals as those presented. But individuals need to realize that everyone has a different definition of what a balanced lifestyle might be to them. Instead of forcing such standards upon yourself, it is important to sit down and figure out your definition of a 'balanced mindset.'

Some might view it as the liberty to allocate time, while others might think it involves just living in the moment and being content with what you have.

Don't compartmentalize

Instead of allocating time to different activities during the day, try to adopt a more cohesive approach. Ensure that your activities are collaborative with one another and do not have an invisible wall dividing them into different sections of your day. The more integrated the activities are the more will there be chances of learning.

The Inverse Rule

The Inverse Rule is a social skill used by psychologists to help those who struggle when interacting with people around them - although this particular skill focuses on improving communication, one can put it into effect here.

The first step is to find a goal, in this case, having a somewhat 'balance in life.' As suggested by the name, we will then inverse our goal, a fancier way of saying, the opposite of what you aimed for. Next, we will figure out ways to meet our inverted goals. For example, being lazy, not having a proper sleep schedule, and an unhealthy diet contribute to being unbalanced.

This way, you will easily name and layout your obstacles, knowing what and when to overcome them. The clearer your inverse goal is, the better it would be to avoid the barriers and move on.

Identify your resistors:

Resistance can come in various shapes and forms, for example, procrastination, not being self-confident, or being insecure. Such things will strive to stop you from doing or achieving anything purposeful. You need to make sure that they learn to grow and overcome them.

Benefits of having a balanced mindset

After developing a mindset that is open to welcome new changes and a balanced lifestyle, it is high time we discuss the benefits of having a mindset with balance. However, the list is endless; let's discuss a few to get the gist of how much the topic mentioned earlier has to offer.

Gives a sense of direction:

Reflecting and thinking over your lifestyle choices allows you to analyze yourself and see which direction you were headed towards, and correct the said direction if needed. The opportunity to figure our priorities, goals, and steps to achieve them helps make an individual more productive and effective in their daily lives.

Better decision-making skills:

We have already learned to identify our stressors, recognize the resistances, and prioritize our time accordingly. Implementing these same methods in your professional life will help decide what is important and what is not – helping in making crucial decision-making processes.

Improves your mental and physical well-being:

Once you have your life under control, it is a given that you start to take care of your health automatically. After overcoming stress-inducing situations, figuring out priorities, and eliminating the obstacles in your way, one is bound to have some "me" time. Healthy eating, exercising, sleeping on time will all be natural results of having a balanced mindset.

Better relationships with others:

Having your life in check and being satisfied with its deliverance will result in a much happier and easily approachable individual. Thus, people will prefer communicating with you much more, which would serve as a plus in your personal life, especially in your professional life. This building of relationships is a way of creating connections that could help in the potential future of job prospects.

Self-actualization:

You will now be more aware of yourself after such thorough evaluations. Identifying your strengths and weaknesses during this entire process of balancing your mindset will help you know yourself better. You will now be able to determine your potential and work around it accordingly – having a better understanding and appreciation of yourself. Although not everyone can reach this level, the struggle of reaching this point alone helps individuals analyze a lot of things about themselves.

Conclusion

We can say that having a balanced mindset is dependent on a balanced lifestyle. If one is bettered, the other improves drastically. We need to make sure that both go hand in hand. These two concepts are an important contributor to improving your life for the better and almost always positively impact you. If taken seriously, having a balanced mindset can lead to a very healthy and happy lifestyle.

Chapter 6
Why Life is Not Fair

There is nothing more discouraging than giving our all to something and then seeing it fail. As humans, we are programmed to crave success. Of course, the definition of success will be different for everyone. One person may work around the clock to get paid. For them receiving money means being successful. Another person may work similar hours but not get paid at all. Just volunteering their time for a good cause and making a positive impact is a sign of success. What we define as success relates to our own personal goals and what we want out of life. Therefore, it is a double-edged sword.

On the one hand, having goals and chasing success is important for a person's growth. If he has nothing he desires or aims for, then he will remain stagnant. On the other hand, being unable to achieve the goal he sets out for himself will lead to disappointment.

When we successfully achieve our goal, we are rewarded with the hit of dopamine in our brain. This hormone is known as the feel-good neurotransmitter because it contributes to happiness or satisfaction as part of the brain's reward system. This hormone is released when we eat something delicious that we crave for or successfully achieve our goals. Dopamine is also related to our levels of motivation.

When our brain is hit with dopamine, it is motivated to continue striving for more. Therefore when we feel like we haven't achieved success, it can be very demotivating. But that is why it's important to remember that life is not fair – no matter how well we think we have planned for a rainy day, something or the other may come in to take us by surprise.

Always be open-minded

One must always embody the belief: "when one door closes, another one opens." Having an open mind is essential if one wants to succeed in life. Oprah Winfrey once said, *"Do the thing you think you cannot do. Fail at it. Try again. Do better the second time. The only people who ever tumble are those who never mount the high wire. This is your moment. Own it."*

We are so used to seeing successful celebrities and millionaires on TV who seem to have picture-perfect lives that we wish we could have. All the glitz and glamor, fame, and fortune seem to come so easily to them. Therefore we grow demoralized when our hard work doesn't bear fruit. However, one must always remember that no one gets where he is without a struggle. We never see or hear about "successful" people before they gain their success. Otherwise, the illusion of their perfectly crafted image would be shattered. But suppose we dig a little deeper into their stories? In that case, we see that they all started from somewhere, and many times under the circumstances even more difficult than our own. However, they persevere and don't let one failure define who they are.

Optimist or pessimist

"Develop success from failures. Discouragement and failures are two of the surest stepping stones to success." This is a quote by the American writer Dale Carnegie, and it teaches us that there are two ways to view a failure. Carnegie

50

takes the route of the optimist, who says the glass is half full. Similarly, Carnegie says failures and discouragements are simply stepping stones for us to reach our true potential.

A pessimist will say the glass is half empty. For a pessimist, the first failure is like a death sentence – that there is no reason to continue going forward with something if one is bound to fail. But if we take this approach, then we will never take a step forward. Our journey will remain stagnant. Our story will never be told unless we turn the pages.

Do not act entitled

The world does not owe us anything – this is something I am sure many immigrants can relate to, especially those who have struggled under difficult circumstances. We can cry about how unfair life can be until the cows come home, but that will benefit no one. The grass will always appear greener on the other side, but that doesn't mean we should give up watering our own garden. The fruit grown by our own love and labor will always taste the sweetest. There will be days when the sun shines on us and days where there will be only clouds.

We cannot sit back and let life dictate us. Nor can we act entitled and expect the world to always give in to our desires and needs. If we want something, we have to reach out and grab it with our own hands. One must always embody the optimist's spirit, who believes there is more than enough to go around in the world for everyone. Hence, it is alright if we try to take our own share from it. The optimist also does not give up after a failure.

Don't give up!

We have all watched a movie where the protagonists are in the grip of imminent danger. They look as if they are about to lose hope, and that's when we shout at our TV screens, "Don't give up!" Their perseverance pays off, and the protagonists manage to get themselves out of the threat they were in. Suppose we are ready to cheer on a fictional character on TV and tell him to stay positive and hopeful. Why don't we give ourselves the same encouragement?

We must be our own cheerleaders. We cannot rely on someone else to tell us to pull up our socks and dust our shoulders. If we want to succeed in life, we need to be self-motivated, and, most importantly, we should know how to forgive ourselves. Many people are their own worst critics – they cannot forgive themselves for the smallest of mistakes.

This lowers their self-esteem and demoralizes them from picking themselves back up after a failure. We must learn to be kind to ourselves. The same way we would support and encourage a loved-one is how we should treat ourselves. If we don't like speaking harsh words to others and putting them down, we definitely owe ourselves the same love and compassion.

Walt Disney is an example of a man who didn't let his string of failures in life stop him from reaching sky-high success. He was fired from his job as a young man and went bankrupt when he started his first animation company. In fact, he had hit the bottom of the barrel and had to eat actual dog food some days just to keep from being hungry.

While such a failure might have discouraged others from pursuing their goal, Disney did not let it stop him. In fact, he went ahead stubbornly and started a company again, and then a couple of more times until he finally found success in running an animation studio. And today, his name is one of the most recognizable ones in the world.

The Beatles are perhaps one of the most well-known musical bands globally, famous for bringing new blood into the industry and their massive popularity. However, they didn't start that way – in fact, the Beatles were rejected by almost every single record label they approached. If they had given up on their dreams, they would never have tasted the overwhelming success that was lying in wait for them.

Conclusion

Life is not fair because "fortune favors the bold." If life were truly balanced and fair, then everyone in the world would either have everything or nothing. It just isn't possible for that to happen. Therefore the simple rule is that if you want something, go and get it. And if you should fail the first time, that does not mean you are a failure or that success is out of your reach. And if at first, you don't succeed, try, try and try again!

Chapter 7
Being Yourself

Albert Einstein is thought to have said, *"Everybody is a genius. But if you judge a fish by its ability to climb a tree, it will live its whole life believing that it is stupid."*

Every person is imbued with their own set of skills, talents, and strengths, and weaknesses. The combination of these is what makes us uniquely equipped for different challenges in life. They can help us decide what objectives and goals to set for ourselves and where our focus should be. They allow us to narrow down what we are good at and what we may struggle with. Let's briefly discuss what each of the terms means.

Skills are what one has learned and acquired through their life. As each of us has had a different journey, our set of skills represents what we have had to pick up on our travels. Driving a car, for example, is a skill. It is something one must learn and practice until he has acquired it.

Talent, on the other hand, is something we are gifted with. Whether it is singing, dancing, acting, or cooking – while they can all be practiced and learned – some people are naturally more inclined towards excelling at them. Such people are said to be "talented." However, we all have a talent; very few people ever get the chance to explore and discover what they are naturally good at and may go their entire lives believing they aren't good at anything.

Finally, we all have our strengths and weaknesses. Our strengths are the things we are good at – skills, habits, or qualities that help us grow and move forward. Weaknesses are the opposite; they are things that are holding us back from achieving our full potential. It is perfectly normal for one to have weaknesses – it shows that we are human and not perfect. We all have something that we struggle with in life. It is important to identify our weaknesses, so we can implement strategies to overcome them.

These four factors, our skills, talents, strengths, and weaknesses, contribute to making us who we are. They identify us and make us unique individuals. They are what help us stand out from amongst the crowd and carve a niche for ourselves. *"Be yourself; everyone else is already taken"* is a very apt quote from the author Oscar Wilde. There is something only you can bring to the table because no one else has walked in your shoes or lived through your experiences. There will never be someone who could replace you. Your individuality is a gift.

Most importantly, people will always prefer someone authentic in nature and true to themselves. No one likes to think they are being deceived. If we put on an act and wear a mask to hide who we truly are, we will live the rest of our lives pretending. Instead, it is important to be true to oneself and capitalize on what you alone can offer to the world.

Self-assessment

It is important to thoroughly explore your strengths and weaknesses and how best to take advantage of them. Where do your talents lie? What skills do you possess that could be harnessed and utilized? It is also important to navigate how your strengths and weaknesses can utilize your skills in the best way possible.

There are many times when we possess important life-skills such as a strong sense of responsibility, good time management, and a good work ethic built upon honesty and integrity. However, these are skills we use in our everyday life and take for granted. They are never given a second thought. They are such important factors in making a person successful. Because one utilizes these skills so regularly, we tend to call them 'habits' instead and downplay their importance in finding success. Therefore it is important to assess and study yourself.

Take a closer look at your daily schedule – what do you get right, and where do you lack? For example, are you punctual? Do you always meet your deadlines? Are you driven and self-motivated? Asking these questions and analyzing your life pattern may give you a better idea of where your strengths and weaknesses lie. Make a list of all the skills in your possession, even if they are things you may take for granted without a second thought. You may begin to see answers emerging in the patterns.

For instance, maybe you are good at cleaning. What makes your cleaning process better than that of someone else? Perhaps it is your perfectionist nature and attention to detail that helps you make sure everything is spotless. These are all traits that would be invaluable in other scenarios as well, and not just cleaning. Our daily life habits can reveal a lot about where our strengths and weaknesses lie. It is important to take a step back and assess ourselves to reveal our positive and negative traits. Hence, we know what we can work with and what we can improve upon.

Have a correct moral compass

According to the **Oxford Dictionary**, a moral compass is *"used about a person's ability to judge what is right and wrong and act accordingly."* In other words, having a moral compass means a person possesses a set of internal values which guide them towards making moral decisions and following ethical behavior. It helps the person make the "right" choice.

However, the right choice does not necessarily mean a pre-planned course of action decided by someone else; the right choice could be the one that is correct for you. Everyone sets their own moral compass based on the ethics they gain from their life journey. We are taught morals and ethics throughout life, whether from our parents, our schools, our religious experiences, peers, politicians, and people we look up to and are influenced by. At the end of the day, they all impact us and help us decide our own moral code.

In other words, not everyone will have the same moral compass because every individual has his own set of beliefs and ideas of what is virtuous. There are some universal evils everyone can agree on, such as murder, theft, or cruelty. However, there are many things that they will still differentiate on. But what is important is to have your own moral compass and to always follow it.

You must always have an accurate moral compass that keeps you on the right path. Your decisions should always be influenced by whether it is a morally right choice or not. Unfortunately, success is determined more by wealth and the ability to consume in today's day and age. Many choose the morally ambiguous path to achieve that form of success. It is important to draw a solid line between what is right and wrong. Not enough emphasis is given to striving for our goals while also not overstepping the boundaries we set for ourselves.

Self-discipline is perhaps the most important factor in maintaining a good moral compass and then following it. It is not always easy to do the "right" thing. Still, one must have the emotional maturity and self-discipline to understand that they have a moral obligation. True success does not come at the cost of stepping over someone else's rights. It will always be more rewarding to know what you earned was not done by harming or cheating anyone at the end of the day.

Therefore, define what your moral compass is. What are you willing or unwilling to do for achieving success? And once you have mapped that out, stick to it. These are your set of principles. They will act as your guide in making decisions and ensuring you are always on the straight and narrow path to live a morally acceptable and honest life.

Practice better investment strategies

Once you have your ethical codebook in order, it is time to start taking concrete steps towards success. One way to do this is to understand what good investment strategies are and start applying them. An investment is something acquired to see a return on it in the future, usually in the form of money. In an abstract concept, one can also invest in himself, such as teaching himself a skill or taking classes that will prove productive later on. However, investments generally refer to buying stocks, property, or allocating money or assets in the hopes of generating an income or providing some future benefit.

There are a broad number of ways one could invest. Still, it is always important to remember that there is some risk involved with every investment. You could invest your money into something but never see a return on it. Therefore it is important to educate and inform yourself on all the different types of investment strategies available to see which one works out the best for you. Knowledge is power; you must make informed decisions to reduce the chance of making a bad investment that could cost you instead of rewarding you.

Better investment strategies must be practiced. Nowadays, hundreds of different platforms have troves of information on the topic, so ignorance can no longer be an excuse for bad planning. Furthermore, we are always investing in one form or another anyway. We invest in our children's future, or we invest in our health. We would not blindly go into these, and the same is the case for financial, wealth, or asset-based investments.

Gain knowledge on how to become financially stable

It cannot be stressed enough how important it is to be financially stable. Being financially stable does not necessarily mean one is rich – it means that his finances are in order. He does not have to stress about money. It means strategies are in place to ensure there is always enough money available to pay the bills, rent, and repay debts while even saving for emergency situations.

No one is born with all the answers. For immigrants especially, it can be difficult navigating the financial nuances in a different country. Things like taxes, tax-returns, mortgages, wages, fees, and bills can all vary from country to country or even from one state to another. Therefore, you must talk to a professional who could help you get your finances in order and advise you on how to become financially stable. These could be financial advisors, accountants, or even lawyers. If that is not possible, there are many free resources available to educate yourself on the matter.

Once you have the information you need, start to implement some strategies. It is not impossible to become financially stable, but it is not something you can do overnight either. You may need to start with steps such as budgeting and living below your means until you reach a stage where it starts to bear fruit. And once you are in a stable position, you can look into investing in the future, such as saving up for a retirement scheme or an emergency fund.

Conclusion

It is important to be yourself because this is your journey, and nobody else will take it for you. Therefore your biggest investment in life should be on yourself – on discovering and improving yourself. You should search and discover what lies hidden within you and how you can extract and utilize it to achieve your life goals. If you become someone who can rely on your own strengths and skills, you will find success on your own merits no matter where you are. Educate and empower yourself with knowledge on making smart investments and achieving stability with your finances, all while following the code of conduct you have set for your life.

Chapter 8
Legacy – How Do You Want People to Remember You?

Humans are social creatures. We have lived in societies and communities since the start of our collective history. Therefore it is very important as part of our social skills to get along with our peers and not be an outcast in the group. However, along with this, there is a desire in every person to be recognized and remembered as an individual.

It is an intuitive feeling within each of us that we wish to never be forgotten. In our own point of view, we know what we have achieved and have been capable of. We have an opinion of who we are, and we want those around us to share in that opinion. We want to be known for being someone important, someone who made a difference. We want to stand out as someone significant who will be remembered for our contributions.

Humans also, by nature, want to be praised and admired. We are biologically hard-wired to seek out care and attention. When we are praised, pleasure molecules are physically triggered to be released in our brain, and we grow addicted to it and want more. Even when humans die, they want people to remember them fondly and praise them.

There is also an ingrained fear in people about being left behind or forgotten. That is why having a legacy is so important to us. The truth is that each of us does have a legacy that we leave behind. However, that does not necessarily mean our legacy is only brought into question after we die.

If we move houses, those we have left behind will continue to have their opinions about us. If we left on good terms, they would remember us fondly. If we parted on bad terms, then our legacy left behind in the area will be negative. Every person we meet and share an interaction with is left with an impression of us. Similarly, we carry the legacy of every person we come into contact with. This means that no matter how small or seemingly insignificant our meeting with a person, we have the power to impart our legacy upon them.

So how do you want to be remembered? Everybody wants to be remembered for the good they did in the world. Rosa Parks once famously said, *"I would like to be remembered as a person who wanted to be free...so other people would also be free."* What can you do to leave a lasting, positive legacy behind?

Pay it forward

People will always remember those who were with them in their time of need. Grateful people will never forget the person who helped them when they needed it the most. On the other hand, we also don't forget those who wronged us or were not there for us when we needed them. If you want to be remembered, it should be for the good you do in the world.

Paying it forward means taking the kindness someone showed you and then showing it to someone else. If someone does something for you, instead of paying him back, your debt with him is in the form of doing a good deed for someone else. This way, a chain reaction occurs where one person's good actions lead to a long line of positive deeds.

Therefore, never forget the help that someone gives you or the kindness you are shown, no matter how small. Always take every good that happens to you and aim to repay it by being good to someone else. Spread positivity in a world where things seem to be going from bad to worse. Mahatma Gandhi said, *"Be the change you wish to see in the world."* Even if your small good action may seem like throwing a pebble into the ocean, even the pebble drop creates a ripple effect, and your actions might influence another.

Be kind without expecting anything in return. Not only will this make you happy, but it will construct you into a person who has pure intentions and is genuinely good at heart. These are the people who will always be remembered fondly by those they have left behind.

When you pay it forward, you may be changing someone's life without even realizing it. It erases ego as it reminds the person that he is not alone in the world – there are people all around us who need us. If we are privileged, it is our duty to mankind to use that privilege for the less fortunate. When we make "paying it forward" the mantra of our life, it alters how we see the world and think about things. Our children will look at us and take inspiration from us. This is yet another way our legacy will continue.

When we make random acts of kindness a part of our lives, they make us feel good and enrich our lives and those around us. You feel better about yourself because you are trying to make everyone's lives better, including your own. You are playing your part in making the world a better place to live in, one random act of kindness at a time.

Spread the knowledge

Charity and generosity do not necessarily relate to wealth or material possessions only. Simply smiling at someone and sharing a positive word with him is an act of charity. It may be all the encouragement someone needs to change his life. Similarly, sacrificing our time for someone else's sake is also a form of charity like volunteer workers.

One of the best acts of kindness you can perform is to impart a skill to someone or share your knowledge. The **Oxford Dictionary** describes knowledge as *"Facts, information, and skills acquired through experience or education; the theoretical or practical understanding of the subject; awareness or familiarity gained by experience of a fact or situation."*

Not everyone can afford to pay tuition or enroll in vocational schools to gain technical knowledge. Furthermore, people in the world do not have access to information that could save their lives or help them escape poverty. Some people are trapped in debts or lawsuits, or modern-day slavery because they do not have access to the knowledge that could change their circumstances. This is especially true for immigrants who often arrive in a new country without any real prior knowledge of how the system works in their new homeland.

When we are born, we know nothing. We rely primarily on our parents to teach us everything, from life-skills to social skills and how to function in society. Without such knowledge, it would be nearly impossible for us to function in our daily lives. That just goes to show the importance of knowledge. In today's world, education institutes have become a business. Students graduate from college burdened with debts worth thousands of dollars. If useful, usable information and knowledge could be given to someone free of cost, it would serve as one of the best gifts.

To create your positive legacy, having knowledge is only the first step. The real change comes when you share your knowledge and multiply your good deeds. Everyone, through their experiences in life, will have skills and knowledge in one field or another. You must really dig deep into yourself and search for what you know. What is it that you can impart to others to help them? You might be able to share sound advice from things you have experienced first-hand to help someone else avoid a similar problem. You could then prevent someone from making the same mistakes you did. There may be some skill you are excellent at, or perhaps you are learned in programs and software that you could teach to someone else.

When you share your knowledge with someone else, the only thing you lose is your time. But even then, your time is being used constructively to do something productive. When you impart knowledge to someone, he can then share it with even more people. This way, your one good act multiplies many times, and more and more people benefit from that singular good deed. You become the fountainhead from where all the goodness came.

Help someone attain financial independence

A well-known proverb states, *"Give a man a fish, and you feed him for a day. Teach a man to fish, and you feed him for a lifetime."* What this means is that knowledge is a gift that keeps on giving. If you give someone money, it may alleviate his problems at the moment, but it will not be a solution. However, if you give someone the knowledge or skills he requires to become financially independent, you have set him for his entire life. This is why knowledge is one of the best forms of charity because it allows a person to stand on his own two feet instead of relying on others.

If you possess a skill that could help someone else make his own living, you can teach him that skill free of cost. He will remember you every time he makes use of that skill. Furthermore, teaching someone a skill to help him attain financial independence takes nothing away from you but your time and some energy.

Making someone financially independent does not only benefit him, but it is important to society as a whole. Our economy relies upon individuals having money to put into the system. If more people are financially independent, they can pay taxes, be free of debts, have more spending money to drive the economy, have more free time to volunteer or work on themselves. The lifestyles and standards of living for the country will improve. People will be happier as they will not live in constant worry of not being able to afford basic life necessities or pay bills or rent. If someone is financially independent and stable, he will be able to put more money into his children's future. In that way alone, your legacy will continue as future generations prosper.

Conclusion

Your legacy is how people will remember you, and it is dependent on how you were with others in your life. If you spent your entire life only building yourself up, chances are people will not remember you fondly. Personalities like Martin Luther King Jr., Nelson Mandela, and Mother Teresa are remembered fondly and with respect today for their contributions to making a difference in others' lives. As the author, Lewis Carroll, said so aptly, *"One of the secrets of life is that all that is really worth doing is what we do for others."*

Chapter 9
My Journey to Greatness!

Everyone starts out small. No matter how great a personality you witness before your eyes, at some point, you realize that even they started from baby steps, from chaos.

As the infamous Ernest Agyemang Yeboah emphasizes, *"We all think of doing something distinctive in life. We all do dream of becoming great and leaving distinctive footprints but, when we get that dream, we must get a clear understanding of what it takes to be great. We must get the real picture of what it takes to live and leave distinctive footprints. We need to understand the real reasons why we must pursue to the end, notwithstanding how arduous the journey to greatness may be and the tangible and intangible costs we may have to pay. We must have a nimble mind, move with tenacity, and dare without retreating. Though we may be ignorant of the certainty, uncertainty, and serendipity we may meet, we must think ahead! Vision shall always be a vision until we take that step of fortitude to make it a reality. When you dream of what is distinctive, make it happen!"*

The climb is slow and painful, and you will, doubtlessly, get knocked down time and time again. But just imagine the meaningful lessons learned and touched with your CAN-DO attitude can make a huge difference to the world. An impact says, "Yes! I was here. This is my work you are witnessing, this is my creation you are using, or that is helping you, this is my effort!" I think we all dream of living a life like that, that even when you leave the world, you want people to remember you, your name, and what you did. Not in a bad way, of course. However, this is not achieved easily. The sacrifices that have to be made are surmountable and staggering. At times, and most of the time, people do not even see you at work, nor do they pause to appreciate you after your achievement. And you need to know that that is okay. That it's normal, and it should not give us a reason to even think about retreating. Persevere and relentlessly pursue your goal, and you will watch your progress turning into an embodiment of your dreams.

Pain-progress

When life batters you down, you don't get the option of staying down. You don't get the option of resting. That's because the world keeps moving on fast; the earth keeps rotating on its axis; people still take their next breath and put their next foot forward; they still attend school and work, etc. Life doesn't stop for anyone. And when you realize that, you will have achieved a state where nothing and no one can keep you down forever. You realize that you have a lot at stake, and no one will come and save you. No one will come and live your life for you or bear your pain for you. After all of this settles in your heart and mind, you resolve to be the one to pick yourself and trudge on. Every time you get pushed down or crumble under pressure, you know for a fact that it's a stepping stone to success because when you push yourself back up, you do it with a fresh mindset, newer resolves, renewed determination, and fighting spirit. And the most important lesson that I've learned is that it is more than likely to be good for you in the long run if it hurts. When you go down, you rebuild with a newer perspective and experience, vital for growth and progress.

Progress-pursue

"Those who do not move, do not notice their chains."
– Rosa Luxemburg

Progression is slow and painful, and most of us fall victim to pressure or failure and give up. Coping healthily with failure and discouragement is essential; whether it's the people dragging you down or life itself, breathe, keep your chin up, and slowly think of a way out of the cycle, out of the trap. If a person puts down their fight and allows himself to stagnate, that's when he makes his first mistake. It's important to keep yourself moving, learning, and evolving because then, you discover what you exactly want to pursue. Once you figure out what you want during your progress stage, you learn to pursue it with all you have. The importance of determination is what gets you through thick and thin; it's what helps you finally achieve what you have wanted all along. So, follow your dream. Follow that whim. Follow your heart. Follow the small voice in the back of your mind telling you to be crazy, to be venturous, and to be reckless. Spiral out of control in the pursuit of your happiness. *"It's better to die in pursuit of your dreams than to live a life without hope."* – Terry Brooks

Pursue-practice

It is a fact that we all learn through practice. Whether it's learning to dance through constant practice or learning to just live through constant practice, the main fundamentals stay the same. Practice, in essence, means to perform consistently, time and time again, in the face of whatever monstrous obstacles one may face. If you wish to invite the perfection you desire, practice is the key to that. No matter how many times you fail or flail, make sure you practice until what you want to learn or carry out is ingrained in every fiber of your being. Implementing this in every aspect of my life proved the fact that practice is vital. *"No matter how much falls on us, we keep plowing ahead. That's the only way to keep the roads clear."* – Greg Kincaid

If you pause and stop, even just to take a breather, know that your only option is to keep pressing on. Failure upon failure after trial upon trial may hit you in the face, but that, by no means, should get you down enough to give up. Know that no effort you make goes to waste; the sweet smell of success will find you soon.

Practice-perseverance

To persevere is the practice of the great. If there is one thing many of us don't realize, it's that tenacity is a vital component for success. Endurance, tenacity, and perseverance can pave the way for anyone and everyone. Without these qualities, you won't ever hear a story of the greats in which they achieved what they did. In the face of the enemy, whether it is another person, another company, society, the general public, or time itself, remaining steadfast and riding the turbulent waves out is crucial for seeing the safe shorelines that beckon you toward success. We witness many people around us having regrets for various things in life, simply because they failed to keep their ultimate goal in mind and gave up before seeing the other side.

On the other hand, we witness many people who failed to attain their goals despite trying their hardest. In their case, they go down tired but content because at least they knew they gave it their all. They tried their hardest, to the point where uncontrollable factors led to the rest of the outcome. For perseverance like that, whatever the outcome is, it is accompanied by individual satisfaction and the knowledge that they went down fighting. They went down, giving it their all.

Perseverance-persistence

As Randy Pausch reminds us, *"The brick walls are there for a reason. The brick walls are not there to keep us out. The brick walls are there to give us a chance to show how badly we want something. Because the brick walls are there to stop the people who don't want it badly enough. They're there to stop the other people."*

If someone really puts his heart and mind into something, he would not just stop by hitting one brick wall. He would not stop even after hitting the second, third, and fourth. A man or woman who badly wants something will get it, and that too, deservingly, since it is a given that he or she will try his or her hardest to get it. Naturally, the people who cannot be bothered enough to see their ordeal through will have to stop halfway or something. It is easy for words to tumble out of your mouth, telling how badly you want something when in reality, your actions say otherwise, and actions are what do the talking in practical life. Thus, the people who merely claim that they desired to reach great heights and milestones find themselves giving up or shrugging and turning away each time they have to face a brick wall. But those who persist, persist, and persist, will make it out to the other side to see a whole new world created just for them, a world where they can be king or queen.

Persistence-passion

The red-hot determination coiled in the pits of our stomach and rearing its head at every second occasion is what can only be termed as one's passion. Once someone gathers the guts and enough willpower to persist and see his ordeal through to the end, passion sinks deep within, nesting and making a home. And it's the same thing that keeps us going even when we feel like we no longer can when we feel like the world is taking more from us than we can bear. We push past all of those barriers and obstructions because of the insane passionate desire to keep climbing, even if it's up walls with iron spikes sticking out, and accomplish marvelous and wondrous things. And those are exactly the things that 'wow' people enough for us to leave our footprint in this world, a sign that we, too, once existed and did something. Something big.

Emily Bronte's lines in **Wuthering Heights** really got me thinking. *"I cannot express it, but surely you and everybody have a notion that there is or should be an existence of yours beyond you. What was the use of my creation if I were entirely contained here?"*

One's existence of one beyond one is a very beautiful concept, and being passionate enough to embody this concept is what many should aspire to.

Purpose -The 'Aha!' moments and positive memories

There comes the point in life where we realize that even if everything is not going great overall, the small moments count. Each and every small moment or memory will build up to something bigger, something more wonderful. And if you can't see them for what they are, you might miss cherishing the happiness and thrill associated with each bit. Now, there are plenty of 'Aha!' moments in a person's life, those exciting and thrilling moments, the moments where you feel a beaming smile break out on your face with jolly laughter following it, that victorious and overjoyed feeling that blossoms in your heart, where you just feel happiness and positivity fairly radiating off you in waves! These moments make you feel like going up to everyone to hug and kiss them for no apparent reason at all. They're just so wonderful, and the effect they have over you can follow you for the whole day, week, or even month. Now, some of us try to find out what causes us to feel like that since these are the moments most of us live for. These are the things that pour purpose into every fiber of our being, that make us exclaim, "Yes! I want to live; I want more, more, more."

You end up wanting to spread love and positivity into every aspect of what you're doing, just to soften the people around you and hope that, one day, everyone can help soften the world, bit by bit. That's the thing. Humans are social animals that thrive off love and softness. It is quite disheartening to witness many people thinking quite the opposite of this, but what we, as individuals, can do is perform our part. We all have a role. We all have to spread love, happiness, and vibrancy. When you feel any excitement coming over you for anything, even the smallest of feats, tell the people you love, watch them rejoice in your happiness, and rejoice in theirs. Love, I've learned, is the thread that can slowly stitch together and heal any broken parts in a human. So, softness, kindness, and love should be what we aim to become physical manifestations of. Noting the impact every small action of yours has on other people will bring you purpose. It will show with every jubilant instant in your life, and it will, no doubt, lead you to become the reason other people might have jubilant and happy instances too.

Chapter 10
Love Myself: How Can You Give Something to Others That You Don't Have

Consumed by insecurities and the need to fit into the ideal types presented by society since the beginning of times, self-love is a concept that is foreign to most of us. Living in an era where this perception is widely recognized and promoted, it comes off as a surprise that most of us struggle with loving ourselves. Constantly nit-picking every little thing, be it an invisible acne mark or that little white strand of hair peeking out from the luscious locks, people often tend to notice the negative aspects of themselves rather than the positives. One might wonder, why is that? But the answer is simple, societies have thrived on people's insecurities, with massive industries being formed profiting off from these uncertainties, making the ideology of self-love almost redundant amongst common people.

Loving oneself self is often mistaken as 'narcissism,' making individuals hesitant to openly accept themselves for who they are. The label itself serves a negative connotation, further promoting the idea that societal opinions hold more importance than accepting themselves. With constant judgments being passed left and right, it is a major struggle for a person to even tolerate themselves resulting in severe mental illnesses like depression or body dysmorphia (BDD). It may come off as a great concern that these illnesses are very common in today's world, with chances of BDD occurring in one in fifty individuals, a pretty high amount for such a severe disease.

The current pandemic wreaking havoc worldwide has left people with intense and terrifying thoughts resulting in irrational fears and anxiety-inducing situations. Due to isolation periods and quarantines, people have a lot of time on their hands to lay back and think about themselves, resulting in the concept of 'self-loathing.' This concept has now been so normalized that people enjoy making memes and jokes surrounding it. With so much hate revolving around oneself, it becomes very important to talk about overcoming this phenomenon. But the question remains; how does one learn to love himself? Unfortunately, self-love isn't easy. It's a hard and daunting process that requires immense patience, don't worry, though. We'll be there with you every step of the way!

Taking out time for yourself

The first and foremost thing to do is take time from your very busy schedule to focus on yourself. There is no best time to do this. Be it going for work, meeting out with friends, or giving a presentation, you must give yourself time to thoroughly evaluate your emotional state. Social activities can be very attractive but very emotionally exhaustive as well. One needs to make sure that these are not interfering with your much-needed "me" time. It is often mistaken that a fun time with friends is the perfect solution to relax. Still, it contributes to an individual's unrealistic expectations and the unnecessary need to fit in with others in actuality. Taking out time for yourself should involve doing something only you like. It could be cooking a meal for yourself, going for a run, watching your favorite TV show, or simply meditating.

Getting enough sleep

Sleep is very important and contributes greatly to emotional stability. However, it is often overlooked by people—lack of sleep results in very stressed out and cranky individuals with very little productivity in them. You cannot expect a sleep-deprived tired person to give flying results in whatever task he must do. People tend to give up on their sleep time to complete their assignments, projects, or work but do not realize how negatively they affect their physical and mental well-being. And on the path to self-love these two things hold the utmost importance.

Exercising

Maintaining your physical self is also another way to promote self-love. People are often troubled about their weight – exercise is one thing that can really help get over that. It helps maintain your weight and releases chemicals in your body that relieve stress and make your mood better. This activity promotes body positivity and is key to possessing a positive mindset about yourself. It can either be an instance, work out in the gym, yoga, or just jogging around the neighborhood – the only purpose is to give yourself time and make an effort on yourself.

Meditation

As the rate of stress and anxiety continue to fly sky high, meditation has been quick to gain popularity amongst almost all age-ranges. Inexpensive and simple, the process requires little in the way of experience. Coupled with the ever-increasing awareness of the health benefits associated with the act, meditation has become the perfect ingredient to add to a self-care routine. Science studies have shown that meditation helps decrease sensory and information overload - a remedy used by anxiety-prone individuals. In that vein, our favorite meditation technique includes sitting or lying down on a comfortable surface with something cool placed on the eyes (cold cucumbers or eye masks work great). Now breath as you do – concentrate with controlled breaths - and slowly let your attention flow to different parts of your body and as they move with your breathing. The technique is a great way to bring attention to yourself, and the sheer fun of this simple exercise is enough to make you fall in love with it and add it to your self-care routine.

Eating healthy

Now we know how much this word reeks of negative connotations for every sane person. Hear us out. It's not what you've been led to believe. Yes, cutting out sugar and carbs is great for you. Yes, eating vegetables helps you get more nutrients and fills your stomach up for fewer proportions. But the thing that most people fail to realize is that we've been tricked by the myth of dieting. See, prolonged states of deprivation aren't any more healthy for you than eating an entire cake. Sugar crashes are just as bad for your body as sugar highs. Eating copious amounts of greens is just as likely to cause stomach aches as eating junk food for days on end. Self-love, as it pertains to healthy eating, is more of a 2-part process. First, one should learn to accept one body in all its glory. As clichéd as it seems, we should learn how to be grateful for a body functional enough to help us live. This involves recognizing both its wants and needs.

Only once you recognize both of these aspects can you move onto the next step without it seeming like the arduous and daunting task it has been made out to be. Let's get this out of the way first - dieting is not self-care. It is not self-love, and not only is it not sustainable, but it can and will result in having a wonky self-image. Not exactly the look we're going for.

So then what? We're glad you asked. Eating healthy simply means practicing moderation. Drawing a line in the sand between soothing your cravings and being a mindless chewing machine. That sounds easy enough, right? Well, yes and no. Although the phrase "practice makes perfect" has been beaten dead at this point, there's a reason it stands so prevalent even today.

The practice of starting small rings true. Instead of making the mistake of reducing every item, you tend to splurge on in one go, focus on one thing at a time. Got a sweet-tooth, maybe buy fewer sweets. Those bags of party-sized chips? Hide them deep in the cupboard. Out of sight, out of mind, they'll stay. Have an aversion to eating vegetables? Make them into side dishes instead of the star player. Staying consistent with small changes will not only prove to be sustainable but will also give you a sense of accomplishment as you progress through your journey.

Benefits of loving yourself

One of the major advantages of self is the self-confidence built through it. This enables you to be cheerful and enjoy even the littles things in life because you know you deserve it. This positivity not only helps you feel better but creates a pleasant vibe around you and everything you do. It also helps you feel more empowered about yourself, resulting in making the best and most correct decisions without regrets. It boosts self-esteem and motivates a person to do better, pushing them towards accepting themselves regardless of their weaknesses or failures.

Conclusion

Self-love involves accepting and loving yourself despite every unfortunate or fortunate event you have been through. It is the process of recognizing your pros and cons and shaping yourself to be the best version of that. These strategies can slowly help build that lost love and develop that confidence that you always needed. Although a very slow process that requires perseverance but pursuing it is definitely worth it.

"I've had to work really hard to love myself, and I won't go back to hiding things about me again." - Er

Chapter 11
Peace of Mind and Gratitude

Most people have to deal with strife, unrest and go through a hectic schedule every day that takes a toll on their mental well-being and harms the peace of mind. Rich people experience just as much suffering as poor people. Anyone looking for happiness outside will not find it.

Peace of mind is only possible through inner calm, balance, and serenity. Feelings of lightness, silence, lightheartedness, and detachment are elements of inner peace. On the other hand, stress, distrust, brooding, and restlessness negatively affect peace of mind.

What does inner peace mean?

People who feel calm, relaxed, and light inside are at peace with themselves and experience peace of mind. People who find time to connect with their inner selves feel connection, gratitude, and trust themselves. There is nobody present on the face of the earth who is not flawed. Those who accept themselves, accept their flaws, and embrace them, enjoy every moment they live.

Peace of mind means being calm at all times despite the hustle and bustle outside. When you learn to accept your thoughts, feelings, and actions in every moment, you can achieve inner peace.

A few valuable tips for you:

- Always be with yourself without wanting to measure yourself against others
- Live in the here and now, without brooding over the past and the future
- Self-acceptance instead of self-judgment
- Accept other people without judging
- Trust other people without wanting to control them

How important is peace of mind?

If you want to find peace of mind, there is no point in constantly brooding over the world's problems and your own worries. Difficulties get bigger the more you pay attention to them. Anger, grief, and confusion strain the soul and can trigger a variety of diseases. Destructive thoughts anchor deep within you. As long as you feel resentment, hatred, or jealousy, you cannot achieve peace of mind. Even when you travel to the most beautiful beach in the world, your mind cannot let go of the negativities which clutch on your soul. If you are filled with worries, you will find no inner peace even in the serene blue sea. You achieve peace of mind when you are fully content with yourself and what is happening here and now. Feel the lightness and joy of existence, set the course to live happily in the long term.

How can you find peace of mind?

Buddhists achieve great inner balance through mediation. However, it is not that easy to find and maintain peace of mind in normal everyday life. Every day new problems arise that cannot simply be ignored. But some strategies can help you achieve more serenity and restore your peace of mind.

- Try to be patient in every situation because patience trains the ability to wait.
- Calm your thoughts and recharge your mind with new energy. Treat yourself to a break in between to relax.
- Don't do all sorts of things at the same time. Just focus on the current situation.
- Live in today, not yesterday or tomorrow.
- Get rid of prejudices and try to open up to new things.
- Do things that are enjoyable and pay attention to your needs
- Be proud of your personality and enjoy who you are and what you do.
- Avoid stress. Not all things have to be done right away - prioritize.
- Meet other people in a friendly and helpful manner.
- Recognize the good in those around you.
- Try not to take things too heavily because lightness warms the soul.
- Be grateful for everything life has to offer. Gratitude is an important foundation for peace of mind.
- Constant stress has derogatory effects on physical and psychological health.

Gratitude - A way of lightening your burdened soul

Gratitude has been on everyone's lips for a long time because it's such an easy and beautiful way to make your life better at the same time.

It's basically just about shifting your focus.

A little away of what may "not fit" in your life towards what is good. But what you may no longer be aware of or just take for granted.

Usually, we only feel gratitude at very special moments, a special feeling that we don't necessarily feel every day.

This feeling of gratitude is also very fleeting. It's just there all of a sudden. But in the next moment, it is gone again. And you are back in your normal everyday mode.

Gratitude cleanses your body from all the negativity that you garner within yourself and helps you unleash the winner's potential!

Chapter 12
Choices You Make

When you tread through the path of life, you are bombarded with options daily, and you are supposed to make a choice. Not a single day goes by when you don't have to choose between two things or arrive at a decision.

Nevertheless, it goes without saying that the nature of choices varies by large. Some of them are entirely innate and easier ones, like what do you want to have for breakfast, or where do you wish to go for your vacations or which route do you want to take to work. This or that? Sandals or sneakers? Cold coffee or hot coffee? Black dress or red? There are lots of choices to make. Similarly, there are a lot of options for us to choose from in various domains of our everyday lives. However, these are small things and only slightly impactful, and we can decide in the blink of an eye. Oh, the simpler times! But then there are the bigger decisions, the ones that can alter the course of our lives forever. Contrary to the mundane situations, some choices can be arduous and formidable within themselves because they are that difficult to make. A part of us wants to avoid them at all costs because, at times, escape seems easier than confrontation. It is up to you whether you want to forgive your cheating spouse and move on or get them out of your life once and for all. Again, the choice is yours, and it is not an easier one. The task is emotionally draining, and since you have to choose between the person you love and the peace of your mind, it can be intoxicating. If we choose to confront the options laid before us straight up, with confidence and courage, we open ourselves to a fulfilling path enriched with numerous possibilities. Instead of procrastinating in fear of choosing the wrong path, the wiser thing is to go about it by weighing the options, study them, do the required research, sleep over it maybe, rule out the flaccid option, choose the best plausible alternative for ourselves, and revel in the chance to design the type of life we aspire to live. The key is to be proactive and plan things out in advance. No, I'm not asking you to plan your entire week's breakfast menu because of "proactivity," but for the more significant decisions, the ones hard to make. While making these choices, adapting the proactive strategy is often found fruitful. You need to be learned. You need to view the options from multiple angles and perspectives. And need to know what you're getting yourself into. Only then will you be able to truly weigh the options, list down the pros and cons, and make an informed choice.

For instance, a student who has graduated high school is now stuck with a dilemma. He wants to pursue health sciences, but he is not certain whether he should opt for Business Management or Project Management. Making the right choice is substantial here because the right career path will be one of the many defining moments of his life. As a matter of fact, graduating college with the right degree will determine the pattern of the rest of his life. But how does he find out which is the right one for him? That's where the tricky part lies. He must gather relevant information about both the programs, do a job market analysis, meet with alumni of both fields, see where their interests lie, and then make a choice. He must plan ahead rather than studying the program that seems fit "at that time." He must know what's best for him and which option is going to give him exceptional returns.

We get to choose consciously; however, our thoughts have a massive influence on the choices we make and the decisions we take. Life is a plethora of choices and decisions, and it is entirely within our territory to select the best course of action for ourselves. But we must be wise and stay put, irrespective of how challenging the choices can get. There always comes a rainbow after the rain. Once all the dark, gloomy clouds are cleared off, the sky becomes a bright blue ray of hope. Similarly, once all the clouds of confusion from your mind fade away, you begin to think straight, and you somewhat know where your head lies. Making a huge change in life can get pretty scary, but regret is even scarier. The choice is again yours whether you want to have a better tomorrow or regret the ugliness that today holds.

In every moment of our lives, we are making choices, either consciously or subconsciously, whether we realize it or not. Those choices determine who we become, what we do and experience, and the results we create. Believe it or not, the choices that we make can make or break us. It would be safe to assume that everything that happens to us is a consequence of our choices. We choose to go to the gym or have a triple cheeseburger, to hit the snooze button or get up and be on time, to have a dinner date with our partner or not. So, the next time you find yourself complaining and whining about the extra five pounds that you have gained, know that it was you all along who preferred the double cheeseburger over the gym. No one forced it down your throat, but it was your own conscious attempt.

"We are the creative force of our life, and through our own decisions rather than our conditions, if we carefully learn to do certain things, we can accomplish those goals."
—Stephen Covey

The choices we make today will impact our lives tomorrow. You hate your job? You need to make a choice between keeping this one, which will eventually lead toward burnout anyway, or switching to a better job that makes you happy. The decision is yours, and you will have to take ownership of it. We often read in novels or see in movies how when someone is betrayed by his partner, he tends to go rogue. He engages in all sorts of deviant behaviors, including excessive consumption of alcohol, drugs, partying, sex, and so on. He becomes irrational, stupid and vulnerable, and pulls off every absurd attention-seeking stunt in the book. In short, he becomes the worst version of himself. However, if we go back a little, we get to know that he had a choice, and he explicitly chose the path of destruction. Contrary to that, the wiser choice would have been to learn a lesson and move on with his life. The options he had were capable enough to make or break him, and it is apparent that he chose the latter.

Having a plan in hand means deciding the future course of action and having the liberty to choose between the alternatives. When we make a planned decision, we are aware of what is to come next. We prepare ourselves mentally, equip ourselves with all the relevant information, get the room to iron out the details, and put our best foot forward. And if we fail, which is only a part of the process, we can always pick out the loopholes and see where it all went wrong. There is room for improvement if we have planned everything beforehand and we are able to successfully identify the loose ends. If not, even then, a plan B is always ready to provide backup. That's the interesting part about having a plan. You are never led astray. Even if failure strikes, you know the alternate route.

Planning is a gap between where we are at present and where we aspire to reach. Planning begins with setting a goal and choosing the best course of action to acquire that goal. Time, as you know, flows continuously. You can't buy it. You can't sell it. You can't borrow it. You can't preserve it. However, you can just use it right now. There are countless possibilities for our future, and every decision we make in the here and now will decide how our future will look like. In some possibilities, one might be extremely poor, destitute, and inflicted with sufferings from the throes that were ensued upon him because of the choice that he made years ago. While in other possibilities, the same person may live a happy, lavish, and well-settled life. Time is just like money, continually getting lesser with each spending. Everyone gets the same 24 hours each day; the only thing that creates a difference among people is the way they use it.

When you have a plan that you know through and through, you have contingencies, too, in case things don't go the way you want them to because a solid plan increases your chances of success. Why else do you think banks require business plans before issuing a loan? I'm not saying that making a planned choice would guarantee you success, but it displays a greater likelihood of that happening.

Life in all its uncertainty has the potential to surprise us in the most unexpected of ways. After all these years of experience in the world, of hurting and falling, getting back up again, it has become quite apparent we need to be prepared for anything in life.

Almost all of us have heard our philosophy teacher quoting Heraclitus, *"Change is the only constant in life."* I don't think a philosophy class would ever be successful without bringing this up at least once. As old as the saying maybe, it appears to be aging like fine wine, except that it's getting truer with time. Let's face it. Uncertainties are a prominent part of our lives, and more often than not, we are expected to deal with a situation never encountered before. Every day is a new challenge, and within every challenge is hidden a new struggle. We are often forced to deal with a situation that we have never even thought about before, let alone plan it. We are constantly evolving, and with that, our life is always changing. Thus, proving that the only thing constant in our life is change. Irrespective of how hard we try to have a command over the future, we simply can't do it because that's how life is. Therefore, instead of fighting life for being uncertain, we must rather learn to embrace it with all its uncertainties. We never know for sure what tomorrow has in store for us. One day, we walk out the front door, and the entire course of our life changes forever. Maybe we run into someone at the newsstand who eventually becomes the love of our life, or maybe we see a job opening at the company of our dreams. The possibilities are boundless. So, we have to be prepared for whatever life throws at us because the giant mechanics of the universe, which make things happen, are always in motion. Anything can happen to us at any time, and we have to act the way we have never imagined.

Most importantly, we must have the financial backing to successfully make it through an uncertain tomorrow. Financial management is an important skill for small business owners or enterprises but on an individual level. The way every financial decision made by the managers or owners has an impact on the company's health; similarly, finances on a domestic level need wise management for the household to flourish. There must be at least six months of salary saved; only then would the person be able to have financial security. The uncertainty that tomorrow brings is all the more reason to have solid finances. You never know when your rainy day would come. The importance of financial management can never be over-emphasized. It is, indeed, the key to successful business operations and living a comfortable life, having the mental satisfaction that your tomorrow is secure. Without proper finance administration, no person or entity can reach their full potentials for growth and success. Money is to wellbeing, what oil is to an engine.

No person in the world or company, big or small, can expect to succeed if it does not have a strategy and relies solely on luck. A strategic plan functions like a road map, clearly outlining the best path for them to follow in the years to come. Whether it spans over one, three, or five years in the future, a strategic plan will assist one in meeting the obstacles that lie ahead. Once there is a well-crafted strategy up one's sleeve, it helps him sharpen his attention to get there since it provides a direction for him to follow. Consequently, strategic planning assists the individuals in establishing the appropriate objectives and priorities and directing everyone's efforts toward achieving them. By taking the time to develop a detailed strategic plan about their future, where do they want to be, how do they wish to get there, etc., they would have a greater understanding of their strengths and weaknesses, as well as their position in life, both personally and concerning others. They would know for sure where they stand, after which they would have a better understanding of the circumstances. Having a strategy is beneficial to everyone in the short and long run. It gives everyone a sense of purpose.

"I believe that we are solely responsible for our choices, and we have to accept the consequences of every deed, word, and thought throughout our lifetime." — Elisabeth Kubler-Ross

Chapter 13
Financial Health and Wellness

We all grew up with the saying, 'health is wealth.' I'm sure all of our grandmas made sure to whisper this in our ears every now and then. Well, the modern world has taken the saying way too literally, and their wealth has become one of the spheres of their health.

Now people must be mentally, physically and financially healthy, only then they can lead a joyous life. They have expanded the concept of health to finances too. If you do not have to struggle with basic life necessities such as putting food on the table, providing shelter to your family, and giving your children top-notch education, your finances are in a good shape. You qualify to be a financially healthy person when you get recreation for all the hours that you work – including infrastructure upgrades for a lifetime without hiccups, emergencies like health expenses, loans etc. All these perks are possible only when you have financial freedom. For me, financial health means having enough sources of income to pay your bills, provide for dependents and save for retirement.

Financially healthy people set long term financial goals and have the self-discipline to achieve them. It does not mean making a lot of money. Many highly-paid people are financial train wrecks while others with modest incomes retire comfortably. Money can be a wonderful servant or a terrible master depending on how well we manage it. The term 'financial health and wellness' is used to explain the state in which one's personal monetary affairs are.

Financial health encompasses multiple dimensions including how much a person is putting away as savings, the amount he has for retirement, and the chunk of income he is spending on non-discretionary or fixed expenses. You know you're a financially healthy person when your financial affairs are in a stable state, and you do not live life from one paycheck to another. Similar to mental health, which is our mind's ability to effectively handle what life throws at us, financial health and wellness is our money's ability to tread through difficult circumstances in life.

If you keep your money in a state of exercise, it will work out for you and make you more by being flexible, and eventually in trying times it will snap back after a stressful episode. You let your money sit around, and it will get fat. It will get lazy, and its growth will become stagnant. Not to mention the opportunities waiting outside the window that it will miss out on. We can either nourish our money in a good environment or we can expose it to hazards, it is completely within our territory depending on the choices we make. In the simplest of terms, financial health and wellness can be described as the sum of our present expenses, assets, debts, worries, values and incomes.

It is not merely a number, but a set of hierarchies and systems, principles and personal values. I'm sure all of us have heard of Abraham Maslow in our psychology or sociology classes. If not, you must be well aware of the hierarchy of needs. Maslow asserted that every human being has certain psychological, social and physical requirements that must be satisfied so they can realize their true potential and reach the highest level of self, i.e., self-actualization. In his seminal work, Maslow organized the human's needs into five different domains arranged sequentially, starting from the most basic to most complex, with each level facilitating the satisfaction of the subsequent, higher-order need.

Similar to that is a hierarchy of financial needs starting from income/cash flow at the bottom, which is the most basic financial need, to investments at the top which are equivalent to self-actualization, i.e., the highest level of financial health. Just like psychological safety, people need financial safety too in terms of insurance and risk management. Once the safety has been achieved, credit follows which is equivalent to love and belongingness. After credit, comes savings, which are parallel to esteem needs, and lastly investments for self-actualization.

In order to achieve financial health and wellness, one needs income to cover his basic living expenses such as food, housing and utilities. Income can be in the form of wages and dividends to transfers from friends or family or even government benefits. It is the foundation of financial security because without an income, what would you save? To protect their earnings, people must insure their money against unforeseen events that might create setbacks.

This requires taking stock of assets, including cash and other belongings, health, and security against theft, loss, damage or illness. To acquire those assets which cannot be achieved through salary alone such as house, car, education, credit is required. In order to get an insurance, people must have commendable credit histories and credit scores so they can access and leverage low-cost capital without hassle. Savings are resources put away to accomplish specific goals.

The ability to save depicts discipline and garners confidence, a sense of achievement, and respect for oneself as well as others. Once ample money has been saved, investments are said to be the pinnacle of optimizing your financial health and wellness. When people realize the dynamism of their economic potential, they tend to invest

97

their money. It is that stage where people divide their money and invest in ventures that do or do not carry risks as well as the potential for returns. Investments are deemed to be a turning point of financial health and security because now people do not have to rely solely on their earned wages, since investments function as an alternate source of income. Investing money in different ventures enriches people with the opportunity to achieve important life goals such as a house in Beverly Hills, or a tour around the world after retirement, and dignity in their golden years.

Financial Health is of utmost importance for very human reasons, because the turmoil of stress of having financial instability brings so much pressure to any person in addition of not even making an effort. It is highly likely that if you can't take care of yourself, it is likely to manifest itself in your relationships in some obvious and some not so obvious ways. If your finances do not allow your plan for the future, then I am sorry to break this to you that you will have very little financial freedom. Ultimately, that's what financial health is all about.

I am referring to the freedom to live your life on your own terms, not by the standards glamorized in TV shows or movies. You may not want the same beach house in La Jolla, but an art studio equipped with your favorite paints and brushes. We have all established this quite clearly that capitalism isn't going anywhere anytime soon. And our passions are expensive. They cost us a lot of money. Many people don't even get to think about their passions, about ever fulfilling them, because they are that unhealthy financially. A lot of people take the construct of financial health for granted, but it plays substantial role in one's well-being.

Being in a sound financial health does not equate to one's capability to purchase something that costs a fortune, neither does it mean a luxury vacation across Asia or Europe. Instead, financial health emphasizes more on one's capability to build strong relationship with money so that one is more in control of his finances and not vice versa.

Thus, your financial health gives you more financial freedom and independence so that you don't stress over times when it comes to meet both your long term and short term goals. It means that you are well aware of the fact and that you have the security to achieve whatever financial goal you set your eyes on.

It may take a lot time, patience, and discipline too, because let's face it, no good thing happens overnight, but improving your financial health is definitely important and possible too. For one's sustenance, mental, physical and financial well-being hold immense significance. As a matter of fact, we're living in a competitive era, both our physical and mental health and directly correspondent with our financial health and wellness. On one hand it holds so much value, but the contradiction arises on the other hand when people aren't ready to talk about such an important aspect. No one likes to talk about their money, whether it's out of modesty or because of a family secret that they're trying to conceal.

Until recently, there has been a culture that takes things for their face value whereas appearances are appreciated over transparency. That Gucci dress? Perhaps it's fake, perhaps it's been bought on a credit card. That starving artist? Perhaps he's a trust-fund kid living parody of bohemian lifestyle. Either ways, there are façades at every turn, compelling some into overreaching and others into settling for less than what they desire.

The harsh reality is that people are pouring money to buy the things they don't need so they can impress the people they do or don't like. Nobody is quite enlightened about financial literacy. The worst part is that even our parents often neglect the idea of teaching us the basics of or even let us in on where the money is coming from. And it wouldn't be wrong of you to find personal finance advice sounding like a condescending parent – had you bought coffee in bulks instead of paying $5 for each cup of milk lattés, you'd have been well off by now! Hence, it is essential that we strive to strengthen our financial stability.

99

Sound financial health, at its best, must be empowering. Almost all of us have dreams that extend beyond our current lot in life.

Whether that is to be a globe-trotter and encounter other cultures or start a bee-keeping operation for a honey farm, everything needs money. A lot of money. And solid financial planning can help us change our dreams into reality over time. When you plan your finances, it is not about skimping – it's usually about asking yourself the question what things do you value the most and what are you willing to give up in the short term for a larger, better reward in the future.

Nobody likes to talk about it but eventually all of us are going to grow old someday. It is a fact we cannot deny. None of us wish to plan for it, but it's almost certain that you either won't want to toil in your golden years, or you might be unable to keep up with the technological advancement or something else may happen to kick you out of the job market. Besides, with increased life expectancy rate, we are now living longer than before. This points toward the need to become financially independent, have a solid retirement plan up our sleeve, and find the best insurance – all of which are aspects of sound financial health.

Once you aspire to achieve financial health, it begins with digging down deep and deciding and prioritizing on your values. Ask yourself, what do you value more? Experiences or possessions? Family legacy or self-fulfilment? These questions may sound easy for now but once you begin to ponder over them, you realize where you stand. Then there's the practical side of achieving financial health – taking stock of your present wealth and tracking your spending, or even installing an app on your phone which tracks your spendings for you the moment you make them.

Ultimately, being financially healthy is about achieving a balance between what your values are. And let's face it, it involves making plenty of mistakes and forgiving ourselves along the way—who knew adopting a horse could be so expensive?

Measure your financial health

I'm sure by now you must be convinced about being financially healthy. Let me assist you with the process of measuring your financial health. To have a clearer picture of your financial health, asking yourself a few key questions might help. Consider this a little self-assessment, ask yourself:

- What is my net worth? Is it positive or negative?
- How prepared am I for any unexpected events in my life? Do I have an emergency fund?
- Do I have the things I need in life? How about the things I want?
- What percent of my debt would I consider high interest, such as credit cards? Is it more than 50%?
- Am I actively saving for retirement? Do I feel that I'm on track to meet my long-term goals?
- Do I have enough insurance coverage? Whether it be health or life insurance?

Answer these questions for yourself and you'll know where your finances stand. If you aren't satisfied with the answers, then let's start putting together a financial roadmap.

Determining your financial health

A person's financial health can be measured in numerous ways. A person's savings and overall net worth is a display of the monetary resources at his disposal for present or future use. However, they are always changing, increasing or decreasing, due to debts, such as credit cards, auto and student loans, and mortgages. Financial health doesn't come in a static figure. It changes based on a person's assets and liquidity, as well as the economic fluctuations in the prices of commodities, goods and services. For instance, the costs for food, gasoline, mortgages, and college tuition might increase whereas the salary remains constant. Despite the good state of his initial financial health, a person may lose ground and lapse into decline if he does not keep pace with rising costs of goods. Hence, financial health is in a constant fluctuation, but you can ensure its strength with steady flow of income, strong returns on investments that you have made, rare changes in expenses, and a cash balance that is on the pathway toward growth.

Ways to improve financial health

Below are the few ways that may help you improve your financial health.

1. Spend less than you earn – it doesn't matter how much or how little you are paid. Make prudent cuts in your spendings, which may result in big savings.

2. Pay off the credit card – do not, I repeat, do not max out that credit card no matter how bitter a breakup you had. Credit card bill is a huge obstacle to improving your finances. If you don't pay off the outstanding balance quickly, you could end up paying more than you would have if you paid in cash.

3. Stick to a budget – a budget will help you keep track of where most of your money is going. You need a budget so it is easier for you to decide where you need to make cuts.

4. Invest – consider investing your money in small ventures which have good returns on investment. Conduct a thorough research, a background check, before putting your money anywhere.

5. Get a trusted financial consultant – most of the people do not have the time, or the inclination, to manage their finances well. Busy with family and work, many people find it difficult to stay updated with investment opportunities and to study the risks involved. In that regard, a financial consultant can help you reach your goals,

Chapter 14
Your Relationship to Money

For now, you take a sigh of relief, and you decide to be more mindful of your finances. You choose to come up with a financial strategy to avoid bailing last minute in the future.

Now the question occurs, what exactly is a financial strategy, and how does it help with managing one's expenses? Well, a financial strategy is basically having a plan for your finances up your sleeve. In an organizational context, a financial strategy enables a firm to assess its financial needs as well as the resources needed to support and meet the overarching organizational objectives while simultaneously designing a plan for continued growth, so the business sustains and flourishes. A financial strategy is substantial to an organization's strategic plan. It sets out how the company plans to finance its overall operations to meet its objectives now and in the future. It helps summarize targets and the actions to be taken over the course of three to five-year to achieve those targets. The prime aim behind building a financial strategy is to maximize the economic value of a firm.

Now, shift the previous stance from an organizational to a personal context. It is not only essential for an organization to have a financial strategy, but it is applicable to each and every individual at a personal level. Put all of your finances in black and white, the cash flow, all the money that you spend and where, label them with tags if need be, categorize them, prioritize them from most to least important, or necessity to extravagant, whatever is more convenient for you, so you have a better outlook of your expenses. Every person needs a financial strategy in their life, so they are well aware of their monetary standing, what resources do they have, areas where they can cut down, whether they need to have more than one sources of income, etc., or they will end up blowing the plans last minute just the way our birthday party guy did. So, to not be a party-pooper, get your finances in order and get them right!

Most people think a financial roadmap is only for the rich. They ask - why do I need financial planning/roadmap? Nothing could be farther from the truth. Rich or poor, big or small, financial planning/roadmap benefit everyone with whatever little money they have. Just like everyone needs to see a doctor at some point in life, it is a similar kind of need with a financial consultant. Numbers can vary. But everyone has income, expenses, assets, liabilities, and risk factors. We all love our children the same, so we need to plan for their future as well. Everyone has goals. Some wish to start their own business, such as a small café or a coffee shop, some want to retire early, some have the desire to travel around the world, and some want to send their kids to a prestigious college. All those goals require money. The reality is, you can only generate so much wealth through your own efforts. Jobs will only pay a certain salary, and your goals are going to require more than a small chunk of your income. You have to recognize that to make these two variables converge, it's going to require an informed, dedicated effort on your part. The best way to make this work in your favor is to understand how you'll get there. These goals often take decades before they become a masterplan. It's far too easy to lose sight of these goals in the scramble to deal with everyday life.

This is why we plan, and that plan is possibly the most important thing you will ever do. That's a big statement, but understand that your life goals cannot be accomplished without this plan, or what would be tantamount to divine intervention (winning the lottery, etc.)? Anyhow, plans don't have to be complicated. They can be as simple as "I'm contributing 15% of my income to my 401(K), and I will always have 1/3 of my income in savings." See, it can be easy.

Wouldn't it be nice had there been a simple trick or a magical formula that would keep our finances in check, so we would never have to worry about our expenses? But alas! This isn't hogwarts! We cannot simply swish that wand and lay out a well-designed strategy for us. We got to suit up, and take the reins of our crumbling finances into our own hands and come up with an effective strategy. Nevertheless, there is no ready made financial strategy that everyone can adopt. A financial plan or strategy, as you may call differs from person to person as everybody has varying income, disposable income, expenditure, short term/long term goals, saving patterns, loans, etc. Don't buy things that you don't need only to impress your friends or the colleagues at your office. I mean, if your current iPhone is working fine, why need an upgrade? But if you have deep pockets, then sure go ahead, by all means. Nevertheless, buy the things you need. Before you swipe that card, ask yourself if that thing will bring you momentarily pleasure. If your neck nods in a yes, then don't make that purchase.

Let me interest you with a few tips that you can start implementing from today to improve your monetary affairs a little.

Add detail to your financial goals – play SMART. By now, all of us are pretty much aware of the SMART goals, or did you skip your Management101 class? I know, I didn't.

Well, while setting up goals, be SMART. Take out some time and don't rush the process. Write down the specific short-term and long-term goals and add an element of time sensitivity to them. Define how long is long-term and how short is short-term. See how long the goals take to come to fruition, and set your timeline accordingly. You may wish to retire early, take a two-month trip to Europe, or buy an investment property. All of that depends on how wise you are with spending your money. For instance, your goal to retire early will come to life only if you have saved enough money for your golden years. Once all your goals are there in writing, prioritize them so you know where you stand. Make a list of your financial goals. It can be as simple as saving for next year's college fees or can be forward-looking, like saving for a house ten years down the line.

Save yourself some money - Cut back on the discretionary items or allow yourself a budget within which you can spend on such items. But don't overshoot the budget because right there is a recipe for disaster in the making. If something is to be bought with a credit card, don't buy it. Follow the cardinal rule for shopping: never borrow to buy. Think before you spend. Always endeavor to save 10% or more of your income. When making a new purchase, be mindful of the quality so you won't be back in the store two months later to repurchase the same item. Moreover, purchase according to your needs, not fads. When you are paying your bills, whether it is the internet or streaming websites, opt for an annual payment rather than a monthly one. The package deal generally costs less. Keep credit cards only for emergency situations rather than for daily use. If you are using a card, use the debit one. A credit card, by far, is one of the most dangerous things a person can have in their 20s. Having a credit card to build your credit score is good, but you should NEVER spend more than you make. A credit card is exactly what the names suggest - you spend money on credit and have to pay it back. Furthermore, don't have more than 1 or 2 credit cards, and don't ever think about maxing them out, no matter how hurtful your breakup is. Also, it is imperative to avoid the minimum balance trap. Pay your balance in full and on time. Interest on credit cards can be up to 40% per annum.

Choose the best ROIs - Always invest in good insurance. Earlier you buy, lower the premium. Begin investing as early as possible. Whatever little sum you have, there is always an avenue for it. Investments should always be linked to your financial goals. Prioritize investing for the long-term as it gives more time for money to work for you. While investing in mutual funds, take the SIP route to circumvent volatility. The higher the risk associated with an investment, the longer should be the time horizon linked to that investment. Learn more and invest some time in reading and understanding the various investment options and concepts associated with it. Always keep yourself liquid enough so you have cash at hand in case of an unfortunate emergency situation.

The 20s is a crucial time of your life, as you just start earning money and start making your own financial decisions. Having said that, if you are not focused on your goals, you can end up making blunders (as you are still learning), which can cripple you financially, and before you know it, there is a debt hanging over your head. Debt is the quicksand that will eat all your savings. And it will stay with you for your 30s and beyond if you are not careful. So, steer clear of being indebted every step of your way.

Have an emergency fund - The emergency fund is vital, and it can protect you from more debt in the future. Situations like health problems, job loss, recession, etc., cannot be avoided as these events are out of your control. Having at least 2 - 3 months of your salary as an emergency fund is a good practice. These are not your savings but the money you keep aside purely for unforeseen emergencies so that you don't have to loan money from anyone.

Be okay with the fact you cannot have everything - You might want to buy all those Gucci's tinted moisturizers, but looking at your budget, you can barely afford any one of them. So, don't be a victim to immediate or temporary

107

gratification, and accept your reality. Know your financial limitations and the fact that you might not be able to get everything you want. Understanding your financial situation will allow you to not fall into the debt trap. Prioritize what you really want in your life.

Track everything - If you don't have a monthly budget, get it now. If you have a monthly budget, that's great, but you also need to track and account for all your expenses. Where does your money go? How much did you spend at Starbucks last night? My point is, always keep track of all your spending and, in case of a debt, have a repayment strategy in place. Some big-ticket expenses cannot be avoided, but you need to figure out your EMI plan and the amount that fits best with your budget.

Travel Plan - Traveling is a new passion for this generation. Even if that comes at the expense of compromising their saving goals and getting indebted. DON'T DO THAT. Again, follow the cardinal rule. NEVER borrow to fulfill your wishes. You don't have to cancel your dream plan but make a plan for it and work toward it. So many opportunities to get good deals to earn free or discounted flights or hotels, etc. If your travel plan costs you more than 8-12% of your annual income, then create a separate account for it as 'LOCATION (the place where you wish to go) ACCOUNT,' for instance - Italy in 2025 Account, and transfer a certain amount to it every month. It will avoid the pain of debt. Your travel plan might get pushed by a few months, but the peace of mind will be so worth it.

Chapter 15
Simple Living and Abundantly Giving

To live is to give, as it is abundantly understood that living just for yourself is merely existing and not living. Truly living requires oneself to be selfless and generous. The joy it brings is clearly nothing short of paradise. If you want to live a meaningful, purpose-driven life, it's a prerequisite that you live for others.

Imagine living a purposeless life, imagine having no reason to get out of bed every morning except for pushing yourself for work, and imagine living a meaningless, empty life. Such a life is just passing the time or merely existing, and no one wants that. Living a vacuum life creates a void in our existence, which is not easy to fulfill.

This void can be fulfilled by adopting the habit of selfless giving. Giving and selfless giving are two very different things. You can easily give away stuff that you no longer need and do not feel even a bit of attachment. Still, selfless giving is where you sacrifice your desires and give away something dear to you. Selfless giving asks for ultimate sacrifice but is the one that gives you sheer contentment and peace of mind.

Selfless practices are not something that could be developed overnight, but the good news is that even if you are not someone who practices kindness daily can also become a selfless giver. Selflessness is also being selfish to the extent that you want peace and contentment for yourself.

There are many ways of looking at it. If you see from a different perspective, there is no such thing as a "selfless act." You either want material gratification or emotional contentment. But selfless giving is seen as an act of selflessness because you have to put forth others' needs over yours.

Parents are usually seen as the epitome of selflessness since they sacrifice everything for their offsprings and abundantly give them everything without a return ticket. The love and affection they shower their children with is matchless and knows no bounds. What drives them to do so much, you ask? What is their ulterior motive behind doing this much for their children, knowing that they won't even get a quarter of it back? What is it that never holds them back from showering all the love and affection? What is it that never lets them put their own needs and wants before their children?

The answer is mental peace. The satisfaction and contentment parents get from the sacrifice are worth trading everything. Everyone craves mental peace, and everyone deserves it, rightfully so. But not everyone knows the key to its lock, or if they know, it's just not that easy to practice.

To be selfless, one has to be empathetic. Empathy is something that brings you one step closer to becoming selfless. But do know that empathy and not sympathy is the need of the hour. Empathy and sympathy sound almost the same, but there is a thin line that sets them apart. Sympathy is just feeling sorry for someone and moving on with your lives, while empathy is seeing the world from his perspective. Empathy is settling yourself in someone else's shoes and see the problem as they see it, or keep yourself in that person's place and imagine yourself as them.

Empathy is not exactly selflessness, but it does bring you closer to the person in need. The other person also feels more comfortable in your presence when you are showing empathy instead of sympathy. Sympathy shows that you feel bad but do not care enough to listen to them, let alone solve their issues.

Selfless giving is not just material giving or donating stuff that you no longer need. Selfless giving is giving people your time and your empathy. Selfless giving helps someone out when you are clearly occupied, but you know that it will make his life easier. Selfless giving is making that small effort to make someone's life an inch better. Even if you give an ear to someone and just listen about his miserable day at work without feeling the need to tell about your exciting day at work is selfless giving. Selfless giving is the tiniest gesture you make to make this world a better place for someone else to live in.

Selflessness does not necessarily have to be a thousand-dollar donation to a charity fund. It's about the will to make even the smallest of efforts. Selfless giving is also not people-pleasing; it might appear so, but it's not. When you help someone out of the insecurity of people-pleasing, the outcomes might be different. Additionally, you cannot carry the act for long. A time will come when you will just drop the act and be yourself. Selfless giving is something beyond pleasing others.

Selfless giving gives you eternal peace and meaning. Just the thought of helping someone out without thinking about yourself gives you a sense of purpose, which is worth trading all material bounties. The eternal happiness it brings knows no bounds. Every human being's ultimate goal is to be happy. Whatever your goal is right now, try to trace it to its ultimate end, and you will know that eventually, you want to be satisfied. And happiness nowadays is mistaken as a material thing to buy because of this capitalist world, but it is not. Happiness is something that comes from within. You cannot trade happiness as a material thing, but you can definitely trade happiness as an emotional thing. You can buy all the stuff and tour the entire universe, but nothing can bring you eternal peace if you are empty from within nothing.

What brings you eternal peace then, living for others. We see a few examples like Mother Teresa. People who dedicate their entire existence to serve others have reached the level of eternal peace we all aspire to reach someday in our lives. Everyone cannot be a Mother Teresa, and we clearly know that, but that doesn't mean we won't even try. We can try to conduct our lives in a way that benefits others.

Leading a life of compassion can inspire others to do the same. Compassion and kindness are considered chain reactions. You do good with someone, and it could potentially encourage him to do good with someone else. But the condition is that you are not doing good to get paid back. However, it's easier said than done. Dropping your expectations is not easy, especially if you constantly do good and do not get anything in return. Killing your expectations is way more challenging than it seems.

Hope is one thing that keeps us all going and keeps us alive. Hoping for good from someone is also a very human thing to do. We cannot entirely minimize our expectations to zero. Still, we should not expect the equal good we are giving out. When we start giving without the expectations of getting back, the level of eternal happiness and peace we have reached is matchless. Mental peace and warmth are something we all crave badly and would trade anything to make it stable. People pay thousands of dollars to maintain sound mental health because that is what actually keeps us going. Living a life of unstable mental health steals all the joy and happiness of life. You just can't seem to enjoy anything you do. Life feels empty, and the void you feel just keeps on growing without any light in sight.

Living for others is what gives you mental peace and harmony. It gives light to your existence and makes you feel that you are actually doing something for the world. The sense of giving out to the world and making a difference is the driving force for a selfless living.

Everyone wants to make a mark in this world. Everyone wants to make a difference. Everyone wants their existence to be felt by others. Everyone wants to be remembered in good names even after their departure, but not everyone can achieve that. That is because not every existence is meant for others; only a precious few can achieve that milestone. People just do not see the bigger picture; they do not know the feeling of living for others. People need to take the first step to experience the warmth it brings them. Just because we all have heard a lot of bad stuff regarding helping others and then not getting the same reaction, we do not even try to do it for once. Or we all are so busy in our daily lives that we just don't think of it as a necessary act to do.

Selfless practices are not something we need to do out of our daily routines, or we do out of the blue. Selfless living could be incorporated into our day-to-day living. Selfless giving is just the small acts enriched with compassion and kindness. Even smiling at someone to make his day better when you are clearly in a bad mood or even talking to someone nicely when he is the sole reason for your bad mood could be counted as small acts of selfless giving. Selfless living and abundantly giving are just the little efforts you make to make this world a better place for others to live in. Giving without expectations allows us to live life to its worth living! Positivities to all possibilities create self-fulfillment.

Made in the USA
Las Vegas, NV
15 December 2021

37725086R10063